THE

RESURRECTION OF JESUS CHRIST.

AN ESSAY IN THREE CHAPTERS

BY

REGINALD W. MACAN, M.A.

Senior Student of Christ Church, Oxford, and late Hibbert Travelling Scholar.

PUBLISHED FOR THE HIBBERT TRUSTEES.

WILLIAMS AND NORGATE,
14, HENRIETTA STREET, COVENT GARDEN, LONDON;
AND 20, SOUTH FREDERICK STREET, EDINBURGH.

1877.

CONTENTS.

	PAGE
PREFACE	v

Chapter I.
THE FACT, AND ITS SIGNIFICANCE . . . 1

Chapter II.
THE FACT, ITS EVIDENCE AND EXPLANATION . 28

Chapter III.
FACT AND ILLUSION, FIRST PRINCIPLES AND FAITH 113

PREFACE.

The following *Essay* was written abroad, and presented to the Hibbert Trustees a year ago, in accordance with certain regulations, subject to which the writer had received a Travelling Scholarship under the Trust. It is now published by them, not (he presumes) as representing opinions or even a method about which a mixed body of men is definitely agreed; but rather because they consider that an open discussion of such points as are raised in the following pages, fairly conducted, can only tend to the better comprehension or at least the more strenuous pursuit of truth, wherever the truth may be.

It is a maxim which the writer has heard stated *ex cathedra* in a German (though, as it happens, never in an English) Lecture-Room, that the student's pursuit of truth should be so unconditional as to exclude any consideration of consequences other than its own success. Such a maxim, the writer often assured himself, lighted him in those studies, some fruits of which appear in the present *Essay*. The wish to communicate what we find of truth is as natural and honourable as the wish to investigate truth for ourselves; but it is often met by more serious embarrassments, and weighted with more complex reasons for hesitation. Such have not been wanting in the present case. But whatever private scruples the writer might have had in publishing this *Essay*, he could not but accept the wish of the Trustees as decisive of the question : nor can he regard it as altogether unfortunate that what so many (he feels assured) in positions like his own are more or less nearly agreed about, but have either not leisure or, it may be, not confidence to make quite clear to themselves and to others, should find here a quiet utterance.

The title of this *Essay* to a place in scientific literature, properly so called, may perhaps be challenged, for it deals mainly with a præ-scientific quarrel. In theory, science only begins where this discussion leaves off. The work is on the border-marches of Criticism and Dogma, and would be superfluous, were the long-standing feud between the powers decided. As such, it cannot but wear at times a somewhat polemical look. The object of war is peace; but even the conduct of war between civilized belligerents implies some common rules or recognized principles. In our theological disputes we seem, for the most part, to be still in a state of nature. We are hardly agreed upon the laws of the combat; we are still discussing the ultimate appeal, the presuppositions of inquiry, the legitimacy of universal doubt, the canons of evidence, the relations of fact and belief. This *Essay* may be of use in elucidating for some minds the distinction between the logical and the chronological order of ideas, and the difference between the historical genesis and the permanent justification of a creed.

To the student, as such, thought and the emotions connected therewith are *ends-in-themselves;* his thought and its expression are the works by which he is to be known. But from obnoxious theories the commonest and safest appeal is not to better theory, but to practice and conduct, or to Truth as a grace correspondent to the whole nature of man. Such an appeal quite transcends the limits of the present *Essay*. The time is still, it seems to the writer, distant, when the effects of what is called "modern thought" upon life as a whole will be manifest. In the present meanwhile, for those interested in theoretical work, is not a fearless and liberal intelligence as great a blessing as for others a creed with all the majesty of old traditions, and all the consolation of supernatural promises?

In conclusion, that he may not be suspected of claiming an originality not his due, he desires to repeat here the special obligation (acknowledged in the text) which he is under to Dr. Holsten's work, not yet translated into English, for the attempted reconstruction of the visions of SS. Peter and Paul; and to add the borrowed caution, that whatever may be the worth of such a reconstruction, the purely negative argument retains much the same force. He also desires to record his obligation to Prof. Biedermann, of Zuerich, incurred as well by attendance on his oral instruction, as by the use of his great work, specially in the composition of the last chapter of this *Essay*.

Ch. Ch. Oxford,
   31 *January*, 1877.

AN ESSAY ON THE RESURRECTION.

CHAPTER I.

ERRATA.

Page 57, line 7, *insert* "to" *before* "him."
  ,, 89, note, line 6, *dele* "or no."

there is one theme in all the range of thought worthy of candid consideration, it is this." So writes the author‡ of the "Critical History of the Doctrine of a Future Life." "If the resurrection of Jesus Christ from the dead be a true substantial historical fact it is of more importance to

* 1 Cor. xv. 17.
† Quoted in Feuerbach's Werke, ix. 297.
‡ H. R. Alger: "A Critical History of the Doctrine of a Future Life." New York, 1871, p. 346.

force. He also desires to record his obligation to Prof. Biedermann, of Zuerich, incurred as well by attendance on his oral instruction, as by the use of his great work, specially in the composition of the last chapter of this *Essay*.

Ch. Ch. Oxford,
31 *January*, 1877.

AN ESSAY ON THE RESURRECTION.

CHAPTER I.

The Fact in Question, and its Significance.

"If Christ be not raised, your faith is vain;"* says the Apostle of the Gentiles in writing to his Corinthian converts. "On the death and the resurrection of Christ rests the whole Gospel;"† says Calvin, in comment on the Apostle's words. "Of all the single events that ever were supposed to have occurred in the world, perhaps the most august in its moral associations and the most stupendous in its lineal effects, both on the outward fortunes and on the inward experience of mankind, is the resurrection of Jesus Christ from the dead. If therefore there is one theme in all the range of thought worthy of candid consideration, it is this." So writes the author‡ of the "Critical History of the Doctrine of a Future Life." "If the resurrection of Jesus Christ from the dead be a true substantial historical fact it is of more importance to

---

* 1 Cor. xv. 17.
† Quoted in Feuerbach's Werke, ix. 297.
‡ H. R. Alger: "A Critical History of the Doctrine of a Future Life." New York, 1871, p. 346.

you and me and every child of man, than any event that ever occurred since the world began." So speaks a "Lecturer on Christianity"* in his "Appeal to the common-sense of the people." "The message of the Resurrection sums up in one fact the teaching of the Gospel," says the Regius Professor of Divinity in Cambridge.† And one broad aspect of the importance of the alleged fact is recognized even by Dr. Strauss when he says that without belief in the resurrection of Jesus a Christian community would hardly have come together.‡

It would be easy to multiply authorities and testimonies, from orthodox and unorthodox sides, to the supreme importance of the alleged fact of the Resurrection of Jesus from the dead. But it will be more to the point to consider directly wherein this importance may consist, and what may in itself be the significance of a fact which is on all sides proclaimed unique.

It might perhaps be objected at starting, that not the Resurrection but the death of Jesus is the central fact of Christianity. It is by the death on the Cross that the Son of God is said to have redeemed mankind; to have reconciled the creature and the Creator. So we read in the second Article, that Christ "truly suffered, was crucified, dead and buried, to reconcile his Father to us, and to be a sacrifice not only for original guilt, but also for all actual sins of men."§ Whereas in the fourth Article, which treats "Of the Resurrection of Christ," no

---

* Thomas Cooper: "The Verity of Christ's Resurrection from the Dead." London, 1875. (P. 1.)

† Westcott: "The Gospel of the Resurrection." London, 1874. 3rd edit. (p. 7).

‡ "New Life of Jesus." London, 1865. (Sect. 97.)

§ That this is not the scriptural but the "vulgar" language, cp. Pearson, "On the Creed," Art. x. § 6.

doctrinal significance is attached to the facts there stated. So it might be said that in the New Testament it is the Death of Christ which forms the supreme moment in his life, as in the drama of man's redemption. It is "the scandal of the cross" which is the keystone of Christianity: "to know nothing but Jesus Christ, and him crucified," the dominant note of the apostolic teaching. The Son of Man came "to give his life a ransom for many;"* his "blood of the New Testament is shed for many for the remission of sins."† "The Church of God" . . . "he hath purchased with his own blood."‡ "Thou wast slain and hast redeemed us to God by thy blood, out of every kindred, and tongue, and people, and nation;"§ is the new song of the four-and-twenty elders before the Lamb. So we read in the first epistle of Peter that we "are not redeemed with corruptible things . . . . . but with the precious blood of Christ, as of a lamb without blemish and without spot."‖ And so in the Epistle to the Hebrews it is in virtue of his self-oblation and death that Christ is "the mediator of the New Testament,"¶ and "by his own blood he entered at once into the holy place, having obtained eternal redemption [for us]."** "Christ was once offered to bear the sins of many."†† The Resurrection of Christ, as an external event, is not even clearly stated, and but once alluded to in passing (xiii. 20). Throughout the Epistle the work and the glorification of Christ are placed in intimate connection with his death; and the most that can be said for the Resurrection is, that it is presupposed as a necessary means and step between the redemption on the Cross and

---

* Matt. xx. 28.   † Matt. xxvi. 28.   ‡ Acts xx. 28.
§ Rev. v. 9.   ‖ 1 Pet. i. 18 f.   ¶ Heb. ix. 15.
** Heb. ix. 12.   †† Heb. ix. 28.

the session on the right hand of the Majesty on high. (i. 3.) And so in that presentation of Christ's life and work associated with the name of S. John; "the Death on the Cross itself is the Return of the Logos to the glory of the Father,"* is the consummation of his work, (xvii. 4; xix. 30)—the complete proof of his love. (xiv. 13.) In the death itself is his victory over the prince of this world secured (xvi. 31; xii. 31 ff), and his attraction for all men: and it is equally the moment of his glorification, of his return to the Father. (iii. 14 f; vii. 39; xii. 27 ff; xiii. 3, 31 f; xiv. 30 f; xvi. 28 ff; xvii. 1 ff.) With this view the Evangelist had to harmonize the given fact of the Resurrection; and it became to him accordingly a momentary halt on his way to the Father (xx. 17,) and the appearances of the risen Master not in themselves necessary, but merely granted to the imperfect faith of the disciples (xx. 29). And so in the first Epistle ascribed to the same author, the Resurrection is not so much as mentioned: the love of God is manifested in his having sent his Son to give life to the world (iv. 9, 14,) and to take away sin (iii. 5; i. 7) by his death, which is the proof of his love (iii. 14). Much is said of faith and of life eternal, but of the Resurrection, nothing.

And so it has been said that the Apostle Paul represents the death of Christ "as above all, the culminating point of the Christian doctrine."† With him the death of Christ is the one and only means of redemption, in its twofold aspect, as a sin offering by which the curse of

* Biedermann: "Christliche Dogmatik." Zurich, 1869. (P. 258.)
† Baur: Paul, his Life and Work." Engl. transl. London, 1876. (I. 273.)

the Law is removed (Gal. iii. 18; 2 Cor. v. 21; Rom. iii. 24-26), and as a death to the world and the flesh, which repeats itself in the believer, in the first instance by the force of his gratitude to Christ who has died for him (Gal. ii. 20; v. 24; vi. 14. 2 Cor. iv. 10; v. 14, 15); and secondly by a more immediate and mystical union with Christ. (Rom. vi.)* And this latter aspect of the Pauline doctrine it is which is brought into full relief, as its essentially true and profitable element, by Dr. Matthew Arnold.† The death of Christ indeed is not merely, nor in the first instance, his death on the Cross; this is but the culmination of the obedience and self-sacrifice of his whole life, and has its significance chiefly as being the palpable sign of these: "the point of Christ's trial and crucifixion is the only point in his career where the Christian can palpably touch what he seeks." (p. 85.) From this point of view the Resurrection naturally sinks into quite minor importance: and it may even seem possible to eliminate the Resurrection and still call oneself a Christian, the words of S. Augustine notwithstanding: "Quod die tertio resurrexit a mortuis Dominus Christus, nullus ambigit Christianus."‡ From this standpoint indeed, it may be argued that the bodily Resurrection of Jesus—or more correctly speaking the belief in it—was the necessary vehicle for the faith in the efficacy of his death, or of his person, or of the religious principle exemplified in his life and death, but necessary only to certain persons brought up under certain prepossessions and superstitious fancies, and by no means essentially

* See Pfleiderer: "Der Paulinismus." Leipzig, 1873. (Pp. 92 ff.)
†."St. Paul and Protestantism."
‡ Quoted in Pearson, "On the Creed." V. ii. 1, note 1.

bound up with the truth of Christianity. In short, it may be maintained: without the belief that Jesus had risen from the dead a Christian community would hardly have come together, but now that it has come together, and existed for centuries, it might dispense with that belief without forfeiting its existence; the life and death of Christ, his person and his teaching—these are what are of permanent and essential importance to men, and not a supposed event miraculously performed on him, and which is neither in itself essential to his "method and secret," nor represented as essentially connected with them in the New Testament.

But we cannot consent at once to assign this transitory importance to the question of Christ's bodily resurrection. His death was a purely natural event; and unless he rose again the third day from the dead, as we may say all Christians have unto this day believed, is not the supernatural character of Christianity lost? Must it not appear that the religion in which we have been brought up, is a purely natural product, which has come to us weighted with illusions, not to say superstitions, the greatest of them perhaps this very belief in the Resurrection?

But Christianity has not come to us by any means professing to be a natural product; it claims to be a supernatural revelation. Here it is that we catch one aspect of the great importance of the alleged Resurrection of Jesus. It is the miracle of miracles. It is the point where nature and dogma cross each other. If the Resurrection really took place, then Christianity may be admitted to be what it claims to be, a direct revelation from God. Nay, the Resurrection is not merely a voucher for Revelation, it may truly be said to be in itself a revelation; to contain in itself a notion of God's relation to nature different to what we could form without it.

But not only is the Resurrection of Christ the meeting point for nature and dogma; it is equally the point where dogma meets with history, and this in a twofold sense. In the first place, if God raised Jesus from the dead, this must determine also to a great extent our view of the historical course of events, of their plan and connection; in a word, our philosophy of history. We shall then probably regard all previous events as divinely ordered in preparation for, all subsequent events in consequence of, the one supreme historical occurrence. Secondly, if the Resurrection be an historical event, it must apparently affect essentially our conception of the historical person of Christ. "In his death he assured us of his humanity, by his Resurrection he demonstrated his divinity."* None of the other events or miracles of his life raised him so conspicuously above the level of mortality, and the analogy of what had been granted to men before.

It might even seem that the apostolic view† of the person of Christ underwent a spiritual transformation in consequence of the Resurrection. At least it is represented to us that not until after that event, and in consequence of it, did the Apostles understand his character and office, and the meaning of his death. In the outlines of the early apostolic preaching preserved to us the death of Christ is rather a difficulty to be overcome, than the great redemptive act and fact itself; and the power which overcame it was the faith in his Resurrection, and the essential object of the apostolate was to be a witness of that fact. (Acts i. 22; ii. 24 ff; iii. 15; iv.

* Pearson: "On the Creed." V. ii. § 20.
† Cf. Westcott: "Gospel of the Resurrection," pp. 122 ff.

10, 33; v. 29 ff; x. 40 ff; xiii. 30 ff: xvii. 3; xviii. 31; xxiii. 6; xxv. 19.) "The ground on which the apostles rested their appeal was the Resurrection; the function which they claimed for themselves was to bear witness to it."* "Historically the Resurrection of Christ forms the foundation of the apostolic preaching."† Even if it is the death of Christ which effects the redemption of the world, it is his Resurrection which certifies it; and how without the latter could we grasp the significance of the former, or separate it from the death of any martyr to truth and conscience? The death of Jesus may be the *ratio essendi*, but the Resurrection is the *ratio cognoscendi*. So it was to S. Paul. The death and Resurrection of Christ are the two indissolubly connected sides of one and the same redemptive process, whose efficient cause lies in the death, but whose ground of assurance and personal appropriation is to be found in the Resurrection of Jesus. (Rom. iv. 25.) And more than this, the Resurrection of Jesus Christ is also the means of his elevation to sovereignty over the community of the faithful, and over the whole creation.‡ (Rom. xiv. 9, cp. Phil. ii. 9.) Thus looking at the Christian "scheme of salvation" from man's side it might seem hardly an exaggeration to say with Mr. Alger, "to the New Testament writers the Resurrection and not the death of Christ is the fact of central moment, is the assuring seal of our forgiveness, reconciliation and heavenly adoption."§

It may appropriately be repeated here, that the Resurrection is, further, the point where dogma and morality

---

* Westcott, p. 123.
† Biedermann, p. 520.
‡ Cf. Pfleiderer, "Der Paulinismus," p. 120 f.
§ Alger, p. 357.

seem to meet each other. The Resurrection is often spoken of in this aspect as a moral revelation, and it is even accounted for, sometimes, as the effect of the intervention of moral laws or causes in the ordinary un-moral course of nature and history. But it has besides this more general aspect a special side for the individual Christian. His life is intimately bound up with the fact of Christ's Resurrection. " C'est un des grands principes du Christianisme, que tout ce qui est arrivé à Jesus Christ doit se passer dans l'âme et dans le corps de chaque Chrétien."* The individual Christian in general finds in the Resurrection of Christ the pledge and earnest of his own Resurrection, and, by an easy step, of his own Immortality; of the immortality of his body and soul; this is a glorious promise for the future, with extensive practical consequences which may be derived from it. For the present, for this life, the Resurrection of Christ is intimately associated by the Christian with the new life which he is called upon to lead. This intimate connection is nowhere brought out more clearly than in the significance of the two sacraments, as means of grace, and in their reference to the Resurrection. This connection is most obvious in the case of Baptism, the symbolism of which is directly referred in the Church service, and by the Apostle, to the death and Resurrection of Christ, and to mystical participation in his life and in his mystical body. The Sacrament of the Lord's Supper might at first sight appear to be more immediately referred to his death; but here again—not to repeat what has been already said of the death and Resurrection being but two sides of one thing —it is a devout belief familiar to many Christians that in

* Pascal, quoted in Westcott, p. 138. This principle cannot however be taken strictly, as is obvious enough without instances.

the Eucharist they obtain not merely the moral support for their spiritual life, which might be set down to the natural working of a sympathetic act of common worship; but also a divine food, which has a mysterious efficacy upon the organ of their supernatural or resurrection life. Finally, there is another aspect of the Resurrection which is of great importance to the moral life of the individual; it is, namely, a spring of joy. The Resurrection of Jesus is his victory, and in it all the soldiers of the Cross triumph with him. There is no other moment in the Christian year so joyous as Eastertide; there are no other Christian hymns so lofty and jubilant as Easter Alleluias.

So manifold and potent are the bearings of the recorded Resurrection of Jesus Christ from the dead. And as it is separately the meeting point for dogma and nature, dogma and history, dogma and morals, so it is a dogmatic focus where the lines of nature, history, and morals seem to flow together and coalesce. It is, as it were, the dogmatic junction where we glide easily from the natural to the supernatural, from the individual life to the specific and the universal life, and so backwards and forwards almost insensibly. It might well seem difficult to exaggerate the importance of such a fact.

Granted, however, that fact and dogma are thus intimately bound up in the Resurrection of Jesus, it might still be asked, is the fact first, or is the dogma first? Is the dogma an inference from the fact, or is the fact—that is the assertion of it—an inference from the dogma; or at least, not the premise and starting-point for the dogma, but the verification of it? Are we to prove the truth of dogma by an appeal to the fact, or to prove the reality of the fact by an appeal to dogma?

Dr. Westcott says: "The doctrines of Christianity

flow from alleged facts. The belief in the historic event precedes the belief in the dogma."* But if we look into the New Testament, we seem to find that the dogma, and the belief in it—to make a gratuitous distinction†—did most distinctly precede the fact. "By his resurrection," says Bishop Pearson, "he demonstrated his divinity." But the Apostles are represented as having already acknowledged Christ's divinity, which might therefore seem to have been manifest apart from and before the Resurrection. Quite at the beginning of his ministry Christ is recognized by Nathanael at their first interview as "the Son of God." (John i. 49.) Even the Samaritans recognize him as "indeed the Christ, the Saviour of the world" (John iv. 42), and Simon Peter, speaking in the name of the Apostles, not indeed by the mere use of mortal faculties but by heavenly illumination, gave utterance to the most unreserved confession of the divinity of Jesus, when he said, in reply to the Master's searching question: "Thou art the Christ, the Son of the living God." (Matt. xvi. 15 ff.; John vi. 67 ff.) In reference to the Apostles we can only say that their belief in the fact of Christ's Resurrection seems to have reanimated and restored their faith in his Messias-ship, in his divinity, clouded and struck down by the fact of his crucifixion. It may be a further question how far the dogma of his divinity was modified, enlarged, and clarified by the Resurrection, as the dogma of his Messias-ship certainly was by the death on the Cross; but that the

* Westcott, "Gospel of the Resurrection," p. 64.
† I call this distinction "gratuitous" because it is evident that a theological dogma is not like a scientific hypothesis—which of course always precedes its own verification, as a hypothesis not as a truth.

dogma, and belief in it, was already there in some form, and that a tolerably definite one—of this there can be no doubt, if we accept the indications of the evangelical records.

But it will perhaps be said: That was the case with the Apostles, but with us it is different. They were convinced by direct revelation, by personal contact with Jesus, by the inward force of his words (John vi. 68), as well as by the signs and wonders which he wrought, that he was the Christ, the King of Israel, the Saviour of the World, the Son of God; but even they required the evidence of the Resurrection—this appeal, as one might perhaps not unjustly call it, to "flesh and blood"—to restore their conviction of their Master's divine personality and office. To the fact of the Resurrection they appealed in their preaching to others, who had not seen and known Jesus; they made it the corner-stone on which to rest the whole faith. And for us who come after, "the doctrines of Christianity flow from alleged facts. The belief in the historic event precedes the belief in the dogma."

Yet here again we must demur. Looking at the psychological genesis of our opinions or beliefs, it may reasonably be doubted whether the belief in the historic event has this alleged priority over the belief in the dogma. As matter of fact our beliefs are not so formed in the first instance. We are born in a certain state of society, and our minds are early formed and furnished with an odd assortment of beliefs in events and in dogmas, and of presumable relations between dogmas and events. It might be hard to say which we first believed, an event or a dogma—probably the latter: but it might be truer and safer to say that we doubted neither.

It must be added, however, that to the child, and to all uncritical persons, the belief in the events is just as dogmatic as the belief in the doctrines which are supposed to flow from the alleged facts. In the Creeds, which we are first taught as children, there is no distinction made between purely doctrinal statements and statements of fact, supernatural or natural, except that priority of position is assigned to the former.

If thus, neither historically nor psychologically considered, can this unquestioned priority be assigned to belief in the event as contrasted with belief in the dogma; still it may be said that, logically considered, this is the proper order of proof; first the historic event, then the dogma; for, "the doctrines of Christianity flow from alleged facts" (*i.e.* alleged historic events). On this view of method it would be the duty of every intelligent Christian, who felt called upon to give to himself or others a sufficient reason for the faith that is in him, to eliminate so far as may be its dogmatic or doctrinal elements, and then to examine, without any reference to any doctrinal presuppositions or conclusions, the alleged events in their purely historical character. If he satisfies himself of the reality of those events, he may then proceed to deduce the doctrines which flow from them: though he will be gifted with a rare logical acumen, if he succeeds in deducing nothing from the alleged historical facts which he has himself imported into the narrative.

If we attempt to apply this method to the Resurrection of Jesus, what result shall we obtain? Supposing ourselves, for the sake of the argument, to be convinced, quite independently of all dogmatic or doctrinal hints and presuppositions, of the historical verity of the alleged fact; to be, that is, in possession of "the belief in the historic event;" what dogma or doctrine can we infer or deduce from the fact, taken by itself?

According to Bishop Pearson, Jesus Christ by his Resurrection demonstrated his divinity. But the Resurrection in itself, apart from dogmatic or doctrinal considerations brought from elsewhere into relation with it, could not possibly be sufficient ground for our belief in the divinity—that is, Godhead—of the risen Person. It is just conceivable that the fact might be admitted, and yet put down to natural causes, or at any rate the possibility of its natural causation left as an open question. Apologists sometimes appeal to our ignorance of nature, and the limitation of human faculties of knowledge; and the appeal may have a good *locus standi* against arbitrary or dogmatic explanations or denials on the part of critics and philosophers. But the appeal is dangerous; for the more ignorant we are, the more limited our faculties be, the more chance is there of any extraordinary and astonishing event being an effect of natural causes, either not yet discovered, or even not discoverable by us. No single event can compel us, apart from prior considerations, to infer the presence of a supernatural agent, either in the person of the being on whom the event immediately bears, or in the person of some being above him.* Taking the

---

* Whether Jesus raised himself by his own personal power, or was raised by the power of God? The former is the modern form of the dogma: The third day he rose again: cp. the Fourth Article. The latter is the biblical, specially the Pauline form of the dogma: cp. Gal. i. 1, 1 Cor. vi. 14, xv. 15, and ἐγήγερται in xv. vers. 4, 12, 13, 14, 16, 17, 20. Cf. also 2 Cor. iv. 14, xiii. 4; also Rom. iv. 24, vi. 4-9, vii. 4, viii. 11, x. 9. ὁ θεὸς αὐτὸν ἤγειρεν. Cp. also Acts ii. 24, xxx. 32. For the first three centuries the prevalent theory was that God the Father raised Jesus Christ from the dead: afterwards, as the dogma of Christ's Deity was gradually developed and defined through the Arian controversy, the prevalent

Resurrection by itself we could infer from it neither the Divinity of Christ himself, nor even that God had been specially concerned in the event at all. At most our minds would be in a state of suspended judgment, *i.e.*, doubt.

With still less right—if possible—could we from the fact of the Resurrection of Christ infer the dogma of a general resurrection. To leave other objections out of sight, such an inference presupposes, in some form or other, the great principle of Christianity already quoted, that whatever happened to Jesus is to happen in the soul and body of every individual Christian. This principle stated thus, not as a maxim or direction for conduct, but as a theorem, or canon for science, is—unless expressly revealed—a pure assumption, which would require to be verified, as for example in the present case by the actual resurrection of Christians in general. Apart then from some such dogmatic assumption as the principle just stated, we could not infer the general resurrection of all Christians—much less of all men—from the Resurrection of Christ. This being so, it is hardly necessary to urge further, that the differences in causality, in circumstances, and in persons, which must be recognized in the two cases, are all so many objections more to any immediate inference of the one from the other.

But it is not unfrequently said that in the Resurrection we have a pledge of the truth of the actual teaching of Christ; and this is urged with especial reference to his promise of eternal life, or immortality. Here we are not asked to infer directly from the Resurrection of Christ our own Resurrection, or immortality; it is granted that

belief became that Christ had raised himself. Cp. C. L. Müller: "De Resurrectione Jesu Christi." § 7. De quæstione cujusnam vi atque auxilio resurrexit Christus.

there is no immediate connection between them. But Christ, it is said, promised us eternal life, and thereto a resurrection; and in rising himself he showed his power and authority to make this promise. Just as his miracles in general were to his doctrine in general, so is the crowning miracle of his Resurrection to the sublimest part of his doctrine and promise, the gospel of an immortal life.

It has often been pointed out, however, that there is no direct or essential connection between the purport of a teacher's words and any miracle that may be performed on or by him. If Jesus had " the words of life," that was to be ascertained by examination of the words themselves, not by calling upon him to perform a miracle in proof of their truth. Here again we must say, that the only proper verification of the promise of eternal life is to be found in that eternal life itself, and not in a miracle external to it. Logically the individual can be sure of Christ's power and will to give him eternal life only when he finds that Christ has given it to him. We need not here enter on the question whether Christ has promised us immortality, and if he has, in what sense he has promised it to us; for his Resurrection would not really be a logical ground for accrediting him, at least taken by itself.

We have been trying to argue upon the supposition that "the doctrines of Christianity flow from alleged facts," and that " the belief in the historic event precedes the belief in the dogma." We saw indeed that this was not an accurate way of stating the original rise of the doctrine, nor yet the psychological genesis of our own belief. We turned then to ascertain whether this was not perhaps the logical order of proof; first the fact, then the doctrine; first the belief in the historic event, then the belief in the dogma. And the result of our attempt seems likely to be this; that the supposed order is no more an accurate representation of the logical process of proof than it is of the historical or psychological genesis of belief.

We have tried to isolate the alleged fact of the Resurrection of Jesus, and to consider what doctrine — supposing the historical verity of the alleged fact unimpugned—logically flows from it. The attempt has failed, for the simple reason that it is not possible to isolate a single fact, or—what is here much to the point—a class of facts, and consider them apart from all presuppositions, whether these presuppositions be based on other facts or be of direct revelation. In each case that we have considered, we were really in possession of the dogma independently of the fact; and when we tried to establish a connection between them, without recourse to any further facts or dogmas, the attempt broke down. We are compelled again to agree with Mr. Alger when he writes: "the Resurrection, taken by itself, proves no doctrine."*

And we have "taken" the Resurrection, that is to say, we have assumed the historical reality of the alleged fact. But this assumption must itself be justified, most of all, if belief in the historic event is to precede belief in the dogma: and how is the assumption to be justified, except by the application of the ordinary criteria of historic probability? And do not the criteria of historic probability already constitute or contain or imply a species of dogma or doctrine? Do they not for example imply some opinion as to miracles? It must certainly be

* Alger, p. 368.

admitted that they do. And suppose we come to the examination of the testimony for the Resurrection with the opinion already formed that miracles are possible, this opinion in turn presupposes another assumption, viz., the existence of a personal God. Thus that the Resurrection should have doctrinal weight and be a source of dogma, it must really have taken place; and must be a miracle; and that a miracle should be possible, we must assume the existence of a personal God. If we now ask for the justification of this last assumption we must not be referred back to miracles, for that would be to argue in a circle; and this is not a legitimate form of proof: and as we cannot prove the existence of a personal God by the mere exercise of our natural faculties, we are left with an assumption as the basis and starting point of the whole matter: in other words it would appear that the belief in the dogma must precede belief in the event.

Now if we, like Simon Peter,* had been the recipients of an immediate supernatural revelation, there could be no doubt in our mind touching the dogma. But the case is not so with us; we are left, as we have seen, to our ordinary faculties, and in the first instance it might seem to their use in the investigation of alleged historical facts. The dogma too comes to us as an historical tradition, not as an immediate revelation; and the problem of the relation between dogma and fact recurs to us: Which of the two is logically prior?

Now the only sufficient proof of dogma would be an immediate revelation—in which case no subsequent facts could affect the dogma, though they might be interpreted by means of it. But it is not pretended that this source

* Cp. Matth. xvi. 17, Gal. i. 11 ff.

of proof is open to us, nor could we discuss any question with a man who claimed to have a supernatural source of knowledge. But so soon as a dogma has been seriously called in question, it loses—at least so long as the question is undecided—its primitive dogmatic character—*i.e.*, it can no longer be regarded as true—it needs to be verified, or disproved; it assumes, in short, the aspect of an hypothesis. As such it has the same relation to facts as have all hypotheses; it serves probably as an explanation of some, it stands in conflict with others: it may throw a novel light on some events, it may seem to require modification in the light of others. In short we can hardly say at each moment which is logically prior in the formation of our belief, the fact or the hypothesis, in this case the dogma.

Yet there is a further distinction which may serve to put the case in a clearer light: we must not confound events and facts—as though the two words might be substituted indifferently for each other. Fact is a wider word than event, including not only events, but also all the permanent causes, substances, or existences in nature. If we ask now, whereto the final appeal lies, to dogma or to facts—which is the same as asking which is logically prior—in the process of proof; we must answer, the last appeal lies to those facts, in the full sense of the word, which are present and permanent, in other words, which admit of immediate verification, which are objects of actual experience. By their light, by the doctrine which flows from them, must all doctrines and events of the past be tried, in the last instance. These verifiable facts are the permanent facts of nature and man, in soul and body, and further, for each generation the actual events which fall within its own experience. Logically the last appeal lies here; but practically that appeal has in general to be made with great difficulty, so blinded and embarrassed may we be by traditional doctrines, or psychological modes of thought implied in the very words we needs must use, or by strong personal associations, or any of the subtle influences which affect the judgment through the will and affections.

We are constantly extracting doctrine from the sum of our own experience, and the experience of others, so far as we can trust it on the analogy of our own. When we become cognizant of a new fact, or of the plausible allegation of a new fact, there ensues in our minds a struggle between this new fact and the existing body of doctrine; either the doctrine must absorb and digest the fact; in which case the fact becomes a confirmation of the doctrine; or the fact must prove too much for the doctrine, and must bring about a modification in the existing form of doctrine, if the doctrine be inconsistent with the fact, and if the fact be verifiable, or certainly deducible from the permanent facts always open to verification. Such is the case with a new fact in the present, but with an alleged historical event the case is somewhat different, for in the latter case there is not merely the improbability of the event having occurred, if it conflicts with the doctrine extracted from the general verifiable experience; there is also the possibility of the allegation being erroneous—proportionately increased the further the alleged fact is removed from the ordinary circumstances and conditions of our verifiable experience.

To apply this principle to the Resurrection it must be remarked that it is hardly possible even to allege the fact without taking, as we have seen, some doctrine for granted. If the assumed doctrine be true, then the

Resurrection may have happened; and supposing the alleged fact to be then confirmed by plausible historical evidence we must modify or enlarge our opinions in accordance with the indications of the fact. To know whether the assumption be true, we must verify it; but is the ultimate assumption of a personal God verifiable? Is His existence reducible to experience? We know very well, without any revelation to assure us of the fact, that it is not; we know that this dogma has itself a history, like all other dogmas, and has passed through diverse phases before arriving at the contradictory *ne plus ultra* form in which it is generally stated to-day, viz., the existence of one Absolute Personal Being. But even were this alleged fact verifiable, we should not be very much nearer the proof of the Resurrection. Granted the existence of a personal God, miracles are *possible*; but there is still a long interval from the logical possibility to the physical reality of an event. If a personal God* exists we can believe that He may work miracles; but we cannot be sure that He does. This belief is also an assumption which must be subjected to the same test as the belief in God's existence, the test of verification and of accordance with experience in general.

It can hardly be said that a miracle is in accordance with our general experience; if it were it would not be a miracle. By the very nature of the case a miracle must break the analogies of experience; and thus in the case of a miracle we are at once plunged into that intellectual discord, that struggle between various doctrines, which

* That a personal God cannot be absolute, if real personality be predicated, is a self-evident proposition; veiled to many persons either by the assumption that Truth consists—at least for us—in self-contradictory propositions, or by an inability to separate metaphor and metaphysics.

we have asserted above to be ever more or less apparent upon the advent of every new fact: the conflict of doctrines, or hypotheses, or imaginations, is only more apparent in the case of a miracle, because by the very term a miracle already contains a doctrinal explanation of its own occurrence at discord with the fundamental doctrinal explanation of natural occurrences.

And as this inner assumption is not only thus opposed to the canons and the data of general experience, but also itself not verifiable, we might be inclined to dismiss a miracle on doctrinal grounds, *i.e.*, on grounds of its *à priori* improbability; and it will perhaps be admitted that this is the general and contagious attitude of the modern intellect at present towards miracles. Yet still mindful of our liability to errors of perception and interpretation, and mindful of the mutual relations of fact (including events) and dogma, and their play upon each other, we may be slow to proceed in this high-handed method. The matter in question is too complex and fundamental; we wish naturally to leave no plausible method of sifting it out of account.

An alleged miracle—and one is enough to decide the main issue—comes to us backed by a certain historical testimony; we must be anxious to examine this, leaving the dogmatic question of the possibility of miracles so far as may be on one side, and trusting to the interaction of doctrine and fact upon each other for a final and satisfactory result. May not the *à priori* improbability be cancelled or reversed, if the historical testimony is very considerable and unimpugnable?

It is sometimes assigned as a reason for believing miracles, that they have always been believed. This fact may help to account for the tenacity of the belief even in the present; but is no logical ground for accepting the belief as final or true. There is no impossibility of mankind's having been in common error, or still being in error on many points; there is evidence that the bulk, if not the whole of mankind, has constantly been in error, and held for truth many doctrines now exploded. There is also evidence that if miracles have always been believed, they have almost as invariably been called in question; and while as a rule they have been believed most readily and eagerly by the less intelligent or less educated portion of mankind, the impulse to believe them has apparently decreased just in proportion to the spread of positive knowledge, that is, large experience representative of facts present and permanent, or deducible from these verifiable facts.

The historical witness therefore to an alleged fact or class of facts does not consist in historical evidence that the class of facts or fact has always been believed.

No more does it consist in any effects, good or bad, which may be ascribed with more or less probability to the belief in the alleged fact. It is a very incorrect though a very common principle that the effects of a belief are a proof of its truth; thus it is said, Christianity has effected such and such things for mankind; Christianity is bound up with the doctrine of the Resurrection of Christ, therefore the Resurrection really took place. Even if the premises were true, the conclusion that follows from them is not that the event took place; for it is an arbitrary assumption, not borne out by the analogy of experience, that beliefs, even beneficial beliefs, can only be produced by the fact which is stated in the belief to have occurred. Thus the historical testimony to the reality of Christ's Resurrection is not to be found in any results, however imposing, produced by the belief that the third day he rose again from the dead.

The historical evidence for the actual occurrence of an alleged fact is of two or three kinds. It consists first of the historical facts which have been ascertained, and which may with more or less probability be causally connected with the event in question. Thus if we are sure that Jesus died, and after his death really showed himself with flesh and bones to his Apostles, we may be sure that he rose from the dead. The other kinds of historical evidence are oral and written testimony. We cannot pretend to have any oral testimony, apart from written testimony, to the fact of the Resurrection; for although Christians have doubtless carried on the assertion of the fact orally from generation to generation, yet such testimony becomes perpetually weaker and weaker; and for us the whole direct historical testimony resolves itself into written records. The best historical witness which we can have for an event is the oral testimony of eye-witnesses, because we can examine and sift it immediately; in the case of a remote event the best direct historical testimony we can hope for is the written depositions of eye-witnesses, or of contemporaries, or of those in immediate contact with them.

In the case of the Resurrection we are furnished with evidence of this kind, and our problem resolves itself in the first instance into an examination of this evidence. As already said, such examination implies certain doctrinal presuppositions, a certain reserve of judgment in general; we cannot escape this dilemma. But we can make the presuppositions hypothetically, in order if possible to bring an extraordinary and logically speaking new fact, if it really occurred, into relation with the sum of our at present suspended opinions (*i.e.* codified experience), in the hope of modifying or confirming, or it may be completely altering them. Having ascertained what it is that this evidence really conveys to us, we shall have accomplished the half of our task.

We have here reached a point where we at last seem to see clearly the full significance of the Resurrection. We have already noticed the many bearings and aspects of this complex fact, not indeed "taken by itself," but taken as it only can be, in relation to the sum of our experience, actual and possible. By the help of this alleged fact we are to come to a clear understanding with ourselves touching our fundamental interpretation of all experience, or as Dr. Westcott says in words of virtually like import; "the question at issue is . . . . a view of the whole Universe, of all being and of all life, of man and of the world and of GOD."*

This then is agreed to be the question at issue. But as the poet says; " the human soul is hospitable, and will entertain conflicting sentiments and contradictory opinions with much impartiality."† Or as the logician more sternly says : " It is one of the most universal as well as of the most surprising characteristics of human nature, and one of the most speaking proofs of the low stage to which the reason of mankind at large has ever yet advanced, that they are capable of overlooking any amount of either moral or intellectual contradictions and receiving into their minds propositions utterly inconsistent with one another, not only without being shocked by the contradiction, but without preventing both the contradictory beliefs from producing a part at least of their natural

* Westcott, p. vi.
† G. Eliot in the Proem to " Romola."

consequences in the mind."* It is indeed to some persons surprising how contradictory and inconsistent interpretations of facts seem to co-exist in the same mind. But they are not generally interpretations of the same fact, and so the contradiction is not visible to the mind itself, which has upon it the veil of an assumption that different facts and classes of fact may be open to quite different interpretations; to a mind, that is to say, blind to the logical necessity of a systematic unity of all natural events and causes, or at least of our knowledge of them. But to us who have glimpses into this necessity, the Resurrection of Christ acquires a telling significance; it is, so to speak, for us practically and psychologically, as well as logically, the "crucial instance" which is to decide our way of thought, and of life, so far as our life is dependent on our thought; it is the touchstone whereon we may prove our faith; it is a vocal event calling to us in a voice of thunder, "How long halt ye between two opinions?"

This then is the full and practical significance of the Resurrection of Christ, and not any special dogma or doctrine to be deduced from it. There is nothing particularistic in this statement of the case; what it has been for one it may be for all. "Quod die tertio resurrexit a mortuis Dominus Christus, nullus ambigit Christianus." By his attitude towards the Resurrection any one may decide for himself on which side he stands, for supernatural revelation and miracles, or for natural revelation and science; for a religion which flows from alleged historical events, or for a religion which bases itself on permanent verifiable facts; for two sources of

* J. S. Mill, "Three Essays," p. 251.

knowledge, otherwise to be called, the one Faith, Authority, Dogma; the other Experience, Reason, Verification; for the permanent intellectual confusion which must result from the inevitable and eternal conflict between two sources of knowledge different in kind and essence one from the other; or for the permanent intellectual progress which may be expected from the reciprocal play of doctrine and fact, of codified and fresh experiences on each other—an expectation which may be expressed in the formula of a faith, as humane and devout as any of its rivals.

It only remains in the way of Introduction to come to a perfectly clear consciousness of the alleged fact the evidence for which we are about to examine. The Resurrection of which we are about to treat is NOT "an internal phenomenon continually being accomplished in the believer's conscience;"* it is an external event that took place, if ever, once for all, at a definite time and place. The alleged fact is that Jesus Christ having really and truly died on the Cross, did really and truly on the third day "revive and raise himself by re-uniting the same soul which was separated to the same body which was buried, and so rose the same man."† Or in the words of the fourth of the English Articles of Religion: "Christ did truly rise again from death, and took again his body with flesh, bones, and all things appertaining to the perfection of Man's nature." Whether this is so or not, is the question to which an answer is here to be attempted.

* Matthew Arnold in the "Contemporary Review," July, 1875, p. 333.
† Pearson on the Creed. V. ii. 24.

CHAPTER II.

THE FACT, ITS EVIDENCE AND EXPLANATION.

It is a fact worthy of accentuation, that there was no eye-witness of the Resurrection. Other supernatural moments in the life of Jesus took place in the presence of human spectators: the miracles of the multiplication of bread were performed apparently before the eyes of large multitudes; the transformation of water into wine was known immediately to a number of servants, to the Master of the Feast, to a wedding party; the exertions of supernatural power in control of winds and waves had the Apostles as eye-witnesses; the raising of Jairus' daughter had five spectators (Mark v. 37-40) who could bear testimony, as well as the child herself; the son of the widow of Nain was recalled to life in public before the city gate; Lazarus, four days dead and buried, left the tomb in the presence of a large company; three chosen disciples were admitted to the vision of the Transfiguration; and the eleven at least, if not the whole number of "the brethren" in Jerusalem, and the Galilean women, beheld the Ascension—a miracle more stupendous perhaps than the Resurrection itself. The Resurrection, like the supernatural events attendant on the Temptation, was invisibly accomplished. No man or woman professed to have seen Jesus leave the tomb.

The Apostles, it is true, conceived the primary function of their office to be their witness of the Resurrection

(Acts i. 22); but this witness was an inference, not an immediate perception. Matthias, as little as the Eleven, had seen the phenomenon to which he was called upon to bear witness; it is not even narrated that he had any special vision of the risen Master: his qualification for the Apostolate was that he had been a member of the company round Jesus from the day the miraculous Dove descended, until the day Jesus was received up again into heaven; the necessary qualification would have been much the same had he only been called upon to bear witness to the teaching and character of Jesus, to the personal influence which the Master exercised upon those brought most nearly into contact with him. There is no detailed evidence even that Matthias saw Jesus after the Resurrection. Anyhow, in the first and strictest sense of the word, the Resurrection was an event which the Apostles believed on inference from other events and facts, not on the immediate testimony of their senses. Even a Thomas might almost have been more incredulous.

But the evidence on which the Apostles believed was almost as strong as it could have been had they seen Jesus leave the tomb, as they had a few days before seen Lazarus come forth. The first believers rested their faith, at first uncertain and timid, not apparently so much on the supernatural powers of their Master while still with them, not on his distinct prophecies of his Resurrection, but on the empty sepulchre and the subsequent appearances of the risen One. Re-awakened conviction that he was the Messias, knowledge of the Scriptures, the memory of his prophecies and promises, of his triumphs over disease, death, and Satan, of his miraculous baptism and Transfiguration, the discovery of the empty grave—all this might have been still insufficient to reanimate the broken faith of the immediate friends and followers of the Crucified—had he not appeared to them in bodily form repeatedly, under various circumstances, and afforded them "many infallible proofs" of the reality of his Resurrection. (Acts i. 3.)

Such were the conclusions to which a simple and unsuspicious perusal of the records available would lead us. The natural impulse is to believe what is told us, what is written, if it does not stand in glaring contradiction with beliefs already established in our minds; and this natural impulse is indefinitely strengthened when a record comes to us backed by the belief and doctrine of centuries, implied and supported by social institutions, presupposed, so to speak, in the moral and intellectual air we are breathing. But that air is crossed with strange currents; it does not remain always the same. We have been furnished, it might seem, in many a case with an answer before we have heard the question; and when we come to put the question for ourselves the answer does not fit at once.

That the records of the circumstances connected with the Resurrection are hampered with inconsistencies and contradictions, was pointed out almost as soon as the records were generally known or read outside the pale of the Church. To the objection to the truth of the narratives based upon this observation, there are two methods of answer or apology. The first consists in denying the reality of the contradictions; it is the method of the Harmonists properly so called. The more thorough-going find no difficulty in arranging the narratives so as to present an unbroken historical edge; none of the narratives, they would say, exhausts the events connected with the Resurrection and subsequent earthly life of Jesus; the Evangelists supplement each other; where there is an apparent contradiction between them, they are either not relating the same circumstance, or what each narrates is true, and any apparent difficulty would be explained or obviated had we other accounts, or had we knowledge of the facts from other sources.

But this apology is a little too naïve: it goes to pieces on the contradiction which it involves, as well as upon any textual criticism, once admitted. It presupposes something very like plenary inspiration; and yet this inspiration must appear wholly arbitrary and irrational in its selection of events to be recorded, as well as in its method of recording them. Why there should be four inspired Evangelists and no more or less; why they should not have shown more or less agreement; why in presence of the mass of facts and words, a knowledge of which would have been precious to Christians, three of the Evangelists should have been inspired to repeat each other to so large an extent, sometimes even to repeat themselves; why the fourth should differ almost *toto cœlo* in his representation of Jesus' life and death, manner and character and nature, from the representation given by the other three: all these and many similar questions will be asked, yet cannot be answered, of the Harmonists. The whole class of difficulties which arise not from the character of the events recorded, but from the character of the records, has gained enormously in force since the naturalization of what is called historical criticism, a birth, we may almost say, of this century. The human element had first to be admitted and recognized in the preservation of the records; in the gain or loss of manuscripts, of various readings, and so on; and many a devout mind has relinquished not without dismay the belief that he had in his Bible an exact reproduction of the original words and expressions of the inspired authors. And what had to be admitted in the preservation of the text, could not long be denied in its composition. The authors, even under the influence of the Holy Ghost, did not cease to be men; there was too much evidence gradually accumulated for the human element in their compositions to be disregarded, and the doctrine of inspiration has received from friend and foe all sorts of modifications, and remains now often but a name, a protest, incapable of definition, but useful as a refuge for minds haunted by the natural need for some ultimate external and tangible authority for the faith which is in them.

But there is in truth no logical halting-place between the doctrine of absolute and plenary inspiration, and the complete sacrifice of the same; and so the more rational apologists have sacrificed it. "As we read the Holy Scriptures," says Prof. Westcott, "with more open minds, dissembling none of the difficulties by which they are beset, claiming for them no immunity from the ordinary processes of criticism, realizing with the most strenuous endeavour every detail of their human characteristics, we shall learn what is meant by 'living words,' what is meant by 'the inspiration of a book.'"* It would not perhaps be an improper account, at least of the most advanced apologetic on this point, to say that it claims for the Gospel narratives no more than that they are natural narratives of supernatural events, the human record of a superhuman Personality. "The Gospels owe all their power to the Life which they describe."

Once on this footing the Apologist may derive support from that which before was his difficulty, and turn the

* "The Gospel of the Resurrection." Notice to the 3rd Edition, p. xiii.

weapons of criticism upon their forger. Just as the Master is now by some exalted more and more at the expense of the Disciples, so the events of his life may be exalted at the expense of their narratives. So one critic says:—" On comprenda mieux combien il fut grand quand on aura vu combien ses disciples furent petits."* And another says :—" One of the very best helps to prepare a way for the revelation of Christ is to convince oneself of the liability to mistake in his reporters."† On this principle all that we find objectionable on any ground in the New Testament may be written down to the human authors, and all that is admirable be ascribed to the Head of Christianity himself: and if any one is anxious to save the miracles of Jesus, he can still throw inspiration overboard, and sink the first Christians never so deep in the beliefs, the modes of thought, the superstitions of their age and nation.

And so we need not be surprised to be told that " If the fragmentary accounts of the Resurrection were such as to yield a simple and consistent narrative of the restoration of the Lord to the circumstances of the earthly life which he lived before, it is not too much to say that the hope which they convey would be destroyed."‡ It is an admission which so far only the more enlightened and candid theologians have made that the accounts of the Resurrection do not yield a narrative which is consistent and simple, though in the present instance the sting of the admission is somewhat mollified by the saving epithet "fragmentary." But, after all, what is the value of this

* Renan, " Les Apôtres," p. 56.
† Matt. Arnold, " Literature and Dogma," p. 134.
‡ Westcott, " Gospel of the Resurrection." Notice to 3rd Edit. p. vii.

new argument of the Apologist ? If various persons narrate the same events, an entire or verbal agreement could only arise from inspiration or conspiracy; but neither of these is here in question; the Apologist discards inspiration, and no one accuses the Evangelists, or the first believers, of collusion or conspiracy. Against such an accusation the answer might be good; if brought forward in support of the truth of the narratives, it is little better than an *ignoratio elenchi*. That the narratives are inconsistent with each other is a reason for believing that they are neither the work of inspiration nor of fraud, but hardly a ground for at once embracing the hope which they are supposed to convey; for there are other ways of explaining their disagreement, more natural, perhaps, than the assumption that the supernatural events recorded actually took place.

It may fairly be said, If various persons report one event or series of events, we do not expect entire harmony and agreement in the details of their narratives: still less should we form such expectations in the case of supernatural events, supposing the latter to have really occurred. And so, had we historical evidence apart from the New Testament in support of "the restoration" of Jesus "to the circumstances of his earthly life," we should be in a position more favourable to the acceptance of these narratives in the main, if not in detail. But we have no such evidence; we have only the account of believers, not of independent observers or critical historians; we have only the result of "inquiries undertaken in fellowship with Christ," that is, writings apologetic or edificatory, not critical or historical. This assertion might indeed be converted into a fresh excuse for the unhistorical look of the narratives, and as such a plea for the historical substance of their kernel; "Uniquement attentifs à mettre en saillie l'excellence du maître, ses miracles, son enseignement, les évangélistes montrent une entière indifférence pour tout ce qui n'est pas l'esprit même de Jesus."* To fragmentary accounts of supernatural events, not compiled by our modern canons of historical criticism, we should not look, says the Apologist, for conformity to these canons; we shall be nearer the truth if we treat them with a certain indulgence and latitude; the truth is the central fact, the details are of secondary importance.

It is however from the circumstances and details that we infer the truth of the fact at the centre; it is from the nature of the details that we ascertain the nature of the matter detailed. If we are to subject narratives of supernatural events to serious criticism, it must be on the supposition that these events are in question, and that the narratives may turn out to be erroneous. We must be prepared to disbelieve the records in detail or in substance if we are in earnest with our criticism, should they turn out to be of such a character that any unbiassed judgment would at once condemn them as unhistorical and untrustworthy. And one of the grounds of belief or disbelief is the agreement or disagreement of various witnesses with each other and with themselves; a certain amount of disagreement and inconsistency may not invalidate their testimony, may even allay the suspicion of possible fraud or collusion; but there is some limit to be observed in this matter; there is a point where divergence becomes as suspicious as complete harmony, and where inconsistency becomes inconsistent with truth. It may be difficult to locate this point exactly in particular

* Renan, "Vie de Jésus," Quatorzième Ed., p. xc.

cases; but even records of supernatural events, however fragmentary, dare not, to speak freely, try our historical conscience too far. If we dabble in scientific methods we must be prepared to find them carry us whither we would not.

The object of this Essay is not apologetic nor homiletic, but scientific, so far as this is possible, where the postulates of science are themselves, so to speak, left in the air, not dogmatically presupposed. But it is inevitable that science should gain a *pro tanto* advantage even in the mere attitude of doubt or question. This is the attitude natural to science, and inimical to supernaturalism: even the very doubt of science itself, is a homage to science, and absolute scepticism is self-destructive. The immediate interests of criticism and of Christianity are not the same; criticism welcomes every question; but Christianity, which only permits "inquiries so far as they are undertaken in fellowship with Christ," must suffer, at least in the first instance, by any of the deeper doubts. And there is a doubt of a grave nature involved in the bare attempt seriously to apply to the records of the events which are generally accounted the corner-stone of Christianity the ordinary canons of historical criticism. It is this attempt which we have now to make.

Probably only those who have examined the Gospels, not with the object of eliciting a harmony but with the purpose of ascertaining completely their differences, have any adequate notion how considerable those differences are. They are nowhere more conspicuous than in the passages which refer to the Resurrection. It may be an ungracious, but it cannot be a superfluous task to point out once more the nature and, approximately, the number of the discrepancies in the accounts we have of the circumstances attendant on the Resurrection, and subsequent earthly life of Jesus; for they are still habitually ignored or made light of, at least by those already persuaded of the facts, the truth of which is just the matter in debate. If negative criticism, which presses "discrepancies," has effected anything, it has helped to dispel "the mechanical view of inspiration;" hence it is curious to hear an Apologist who speaks of the Evangelists as "writers who simply say the truth to the best of their power in the ordinary language of common life," saying of a criticism which attempts to find out how far this power of the Evangelists to say the truth simply extends, and what exactly is the truth of what they say, that "such criticism scarcely deserves serious notice." It is not however merely "the mechanical view of inspiration" which Apologists will have to abandon, as some of them have already done, but other mechanical views, of truth, for example, as "handed down:" and to persons who do not start from a dogmatic necessity, the discovery that the Evangelists are "writers who simply say the truth to the best of their powers in the ordinary language of common life," looks like a rather late assumption, though veiled with a show of critical candour. And it must be remembered that criticism, though it may start from an examination of the narratives, and in its boyhood find and press "discrepancies" in them as grounds for suspecting their truth, is far from tarrying there amid the narratives and their "discrepancies;" it also attempts an explanation, it also can say "the phenomena presented by the narratives are exactly such as we should expect," without the assumption that the phenomena detailed in the narratives took place exactly as they are there represented to have taken place, or took place, some of them, at all.

In outline the circumstances attending the Resurrection were as follows:—On coming to the grave in the morning of the first day of the week, where two nights before they had seen the dead body of their Master deposited, the Galilean women found the sepulchre empty: a vision of angels assured them that Jesus had risen from the tomb; and bade them go tell the Apostles of the fact. The news having come to the Apostles' ears, some of them assured themselves of the fact that the grave was indeed empty; and the idea that Jesus was of a surety again alive was confirmed by his several appearances to disciples, alone and together, on that first day of the week; and was put beyond question by repeated intercourse with him, by sensual contact, under various circumstances, in various places, during a period of forty days, until in the presence of his Apostles he was taken up visibly into heaven from a spot in the neighbourhood of Jerusalem. Such is the bare outline, or thread which runs through the narratives; but even here we encounter difficulties which amount to considerable "discrepancies" to say the least. From the narratives how are we to answer such questions as the following: Did Jesus himself appear to the women, or to any of them, or had they only "a vision of angels?" Did Jesus ascend to heaven on the same day on which he rose from the dead, or forty days later? Did he ascend from Bethany or from Galilee? Did he ascend at all, and was the Ascension (not clearly described in any of the Gospels), an event distinct from the Resurrection? If we proceed to details, we are at once involved in inextricable confusion. "The *lacunæ*, the compressions, the variations, the actual differences, the subjectivity of the narrators as affected by spiritual revelations, render all harmonies at best uncertain." But nothing disguises the incoherence of the narratives severally and all together save a silent assumption of their coherence—an assumption which must be based on doctrinal considerations foreign to the simple canons of historical criticism which we apply to profane historians, for it could scarcely be the result, much less the presupposition of an examination of the narratives, in which due weight was accorded to "discrepancies" and contradictions.

All the evangelical records start from the fact that the grave was found empty, and they all agree further that this discovery was not made in the first instance by the Apostles. But they do not agree in the names or number of the women who visited the sepulchre, nor in the time, nor in the object of the visit, nor in what they saw when they reached the sepulchre. According to Matthew the visit to the sepulchre takes place late on Saturday night—as we should say—according to the other Evangelists early on Sunday morning, "after sunrise" Marks adds; "while it was still dusk," says. S. John.* That no harmony is here possible by the supposition of two or more visits of the women is proved negatively, by the fact that none of the Evangelists say anything about two visits of the *women;* positively, by the fact that according to Matthew the Resurrection has already taken place on Saturday night—in which case it would be impossible for the Maries to go through the scenes narrated by the other Evangelists on the following morning. According

---

* There is no need to press the discrepancy between Mark and John as to the time of the visit, to which Dr. Farrar has such a triumphant answer ready; but it is curious that he singles this one out as a model of "boyish verbal criticism," and says nothing about the contradiction between Matthew and the other Evangelists.—"Life of Christ," 13th Ed. II., 431 f. notes.

to Matthew the visit is paid by the two Maries; according to Luke by several women (xxiii. 55, xxiv. 1-10), according to Mark by three, two of them the same as those named by Luke, the third not Johanna but Salome; according to John, Mary Magdalene goes alone. There is an intimation of the possible presence of other women, in the plural used in John, xxii. 2:—but this does not help us to a harmony of his narrative with the Synoptic narrative, for it is impossible to find room in the latter for the separate action of Mary Magdalene, or in the fourth Gospel for the combined action of the other women. The object of the women's visit is also variously stated, and the various statements involve a "discrepancy" which amounts pretty nigh to a contradiction. According to Matthew the two Maries, according to John the one Mary visited the tomb merely to see it, or the body; which John informs us was already embalmed in the Jewish mode, and with expense surpassing that lavished on kingly corpses. According to Luke and Mark the women came with the intention of embalming the corpse—to do over again what they had already seen sumptuously done two nights before (cf. Matt. xxvii. 57-61; Mark xx. 47; Luke xxiii. 55-56; John xix. 38-42.)* What they witness on arriving at the grave is no less variously narrated. According to Matthew it would appear that they beheld the descent of the Angel from heaven, and saw him roll away the stone; according to the other three accounts they find the stone already removed before their arrival. There is a further discrepancy in the number of the Angels at the sepulchre—in their positions, and their

* With the further "discrepancy" that, according to Luke, the women had prepared spices before starting for the tomb; according to Mark they bought them on Sunday morning.

words to the women. John mentions no Angel appearance in the first visit to the tomb; Matthew says there was one Angel outside the grave, sitting on the stone; Mark, one Angel inside the grave, sitting; Luke, two Angels outside the grave, standing. According to Matthew and Mark, the angelic message contains a command to go and inform the Apostles of his Resurrection; Luke does not mention this command, but states that the women as a matter of fact went and informed the Apostles—a statement irreconcilable with Mark xvi. 8. Matthew adds a command to the Apostles to go into Galilee to meet the risen Master; Luke says nothing of the command, but he makes the Angel mention Galilee in a substantially different context. The subsequent conduct of the women is equally variously narrated. According to John, Mary Magdalene goes to Simon Peter and "the other disciple," and informs them that the body is no longer in the grave, but says nothing of Resurrection or angelic messengers: according to Luke, the women returned from the sepulchre and narrated everything to the Eleven " and the rest;" according to Mark, they fled from the sepulchre and told nobody anything at all; according to Matthew, they ran to bear the news and message to the disciples, and were met by Jesus on the way, embraced his feet, and received from him over again the directions which he had a few minutes before conveyed to them by his Angel!* Between the first appearance of the risen Jesus to the two Maries as narrated by Matthew, and the first appearance of the risen Jesus to the one Mary as narrated by John, there is not merely

* Unless indeed we lay stress upon "my brethren," and suppose that the Angel had delivered his message incompletely.

"a discrepancy," there is an irreconcilable contradiction. Both may be false—Luke says nothing of either—but both cannot be true.

We have now come so far in the narrative, that, somehow or other, apparently on Sunday morning, news is brought to the disciples that the grave of their Master is empty. They are not the only persons in Jerusalem to whom this news is brought, for according to Matthew the rulers have already become acquainted with all the circumstances on the testimony of the soldiers who had been set to guard the tomb. But how differently the rulers and the disciples receive the news! The rulers display no suspicion of the reality of the Resurrection and angelic visitation—Sadducees though they were: the Apostles regard the story of the women as "idle tales," and they believed them not. Peter however, to whom a special message had been sent (Mark xvi. 7), visits the tomb (Luke xxiv. 12), and his example is followed by others (Luke xxiv. 24). We are met here by a fresh discrepancy; did Peter go alone, as Luke implies, or in company with "the other disciple," as John says? That Luke and John are only relating one and the same visit of Peter is put beyond doubt, not merely by the general consideration of the difficulty of two such visits, and the necessity of each of them being Peter's first visit, but also by a comparison of the language of the narratives in both cases, as already given in the fifth Wolfenbüttler Fragment.*

---

* Fragmente des Wolfenbüttelschen Ungenannten, Bekanntgemacht von G. E. Lessing, p. 274 (Ed. 1788. Berlin).

Luke xxiv. 12. Peter ran, $\check{\epsilon}\delta\rho\alpha\mu\epsilon\nu$. John xx. 4, they (Peter and John) ran, $\check{\epsilon}\tau\rho\epsilon\chi o\nu$.

its Evidence and Explanation. 43

Such is a brief analysis and comparison of the evangelical records so far as concerns the first of the two great "moments" on which the belief in the Resurrection of Jesus is founded, viz., the discovery of the empty grave. Taken by itself indeed the empty grave could not prove the Resurrection; but then we are furnished with the angelic explanations, "He is not here, he is risen." Do we believe in the existence of Angels, and if so, on what ground? On the ground of any present or verifiable experience, or on the ground of tradition? On the ground of scientific records, or of narratives such as the one at present under discussion? But even if we believe in Angels, are the narratives of their appearance in the present case such as to justify us in accepting the accounts as trustworthy? If the question were merely whether some men had appeared at a particular time and place and made certain statements, would the alleged fact be admitted on evidence so discrepant and fragmentary as the evangelical records of the angelic appearances at the empty sepulchre? Is it so much as certain that the women, that the Apostles, really found the sepulchre empty? Is it perfectly certain that Jesus was buried in the place and manner described?

These are questions, the consideration of which may be appropriately postponed until we have discussed the other great "moment" in the proof of the Resurrection

Luke xxiv. 12. Peter stooping down (παρακύψας). John xx. 5, John stooping down (παρακύψας).

Luke xxiv. 12. Peter beheld the linen clothes laid by themselves (βλέπει τὰ ὀθόνια κείμενα μόνα). John xx. 6, 7. Peter seeth the linen clothes lie, And the napkin . . . . not lying with the linen clothes (θεωρεῖ τὰ ὀθόνια κείμενα καὶ τὸ σουδάριον οὐ μετὰ τῶν ὀθονίων κείμενον).

Luke xxiv. 12. Peter went away home (ἀπῆλθε πρὸς ἑαυτόν). John xx. 10. Peter and John went home (ἀπῆλθον πάλιν πρὸς ἑαυτούς).

of Jesus, viz., his appearances. This might be called the positive, as the empty grave is the negative, argument for the fact of the Resurrection. They belong to each other, but not indissolubly; they might both or neither be matter of fact; or one might be matter of fact and the other not. We shall be in a better position to decide on both, when we have reviewed the whole argument, the whole narrative and the theory, or theories, connected with it.

The Christophanies, or appearances of Jesus after his death, as recorded by the Evangelists, may be roughly discriminated according to the persons to whom, and according to the places where, he appeared: that is, according as he appeared to men or women; and according as he appeared in Jerusalem and the neighbourhood, or in Galilee.

The first and fourth Evangelists alone give any details of a Christophany to women, but the second, in the form in which we have his gospel, mentions curtly the fact that "when Jesus was risen early the first day of the week, he appeared first to Mary Magdalene." (Mark xvi. 9.) The first appearance mentioned by the fourth gospel is also to Mary Magdalene; and so far there is an agreement between the second and fourth gospels: but how are we to reconcile the rest of their narratives? The last twelve verses of the second gospel are not indeed authentic, but they are canonical, and in any case enshrine probably a primitive tradition.* Without pressing the "discrepancy" which results from a comparison of the first eight verses of Mark xvi. with the three verses following (9-11)—there is still a difficulty in

---

* Cf. Farrar, "Life of Christ," II. 434, note.

its Evidence and Explanation. 45

identifying as to place, time, and circumstances the appearance to Mary mentioned by Mark, with the appearance to Mary described by John, and the difficulty is augmented when we take into account the narrative of Matthew, according to which Jesus appeared to the women, that is to the two Maries, before they had communicated the news of the empty sepulchre to anybody. According to John, Mary Magdalene brings word to Peter and "the other disciple" that the grave is empty; according to Mark she brings word to "them that had been with him" of an appearance to her. Is this appearance the same as that referred by John to her second visit to the sepulchre? But what then are we to make of the appearance to her and the other Mary on their way from the sepulchre to tell the disciples in the first instance, as narrated by Matthew? Is the appearance, Mark xvi. 9, the same as that narrated by Matthew xxviii. 9? But what then are we to make—not merely of Mark's omission of the other Mary, but of John's narrative? If Mark and John are correct, then it might be that Jesus appeared to Mary alone on the occasion of a second visit to the empty sepulchre: though in this case we could not easily identify the first visit narrated by John with the first visit narrated by Mark (xvi. 1-8). If Matthew and Mark were both correct, then the appearance mentioned, Mark xvi. 9, might be identified with the appearance, Matt. xxviii. 9, in spite of the omission of all mention of the other Mary in the former passage— which seems to bring it nearer to John's narrative.* But

---

* A good instance of the way "the perfect *possible* coherence" of the narratives may be "silently" shown is to be found in Dr. Farrar's treatment of the conflicting accounts of the Evangelists as to the conduct of the women on leaving the sepulchre. Matthew

if all three narratives are correct what silent assumptions will help us out of the maze of discrepancies? How many appearances were granted to Mary Magdalene? She may have had two, but she cannot have had two first appearances. There is no room for a separate appearance to her, as narrated by John, before the appearance to her in company with the other Mary, narrated by Matthew; on the other hand, if Mary had already had on her way back from the sepulchre the first time an appearance of Christ, as narrated by Matthew, what are we to say of John's narrative of her coming to Peter and the other disciple merely with the announcement, " they have taken away the Lord out of the sepulchre, and we know not where they have laid him?"

Luke only increases our perplexity, for he not only omits all mention of a Christophany to the women, but his narrative implies that, so far as he knew, there had been none. Luke xxiv. 23, 24, cp. Luke i. 1-4. It is remarkable that S. Paul in giving a list of the Christophanies (1 Cor. xv.) says nothing of any appearance to any woman, *i.e.*, omits what, according to the Evangelists, was the first appearance, were perhaps the first appearances of all. The Pauline list we shall come to consider later, in its details: but this omission in the earliest and most authentic record which we possess, taken in connection with the discordant characters of

says they ran to bring the disciples word (xxviii. 8, cf. 16), which implies that they delivered their message. Luke says expressly that they returned from the sepulchre, and told all these things to the Eleven and to all the rest (xxiv. 9). Mark says they fled from the sepulchre, and said nothing to any man (xvi. 8). Dr. Farrar says, "They hurried back in a tumult of rapture and alarm, telling no one except the disciples." ("Life of Christ," II., 432.) As if this exception were quite in the spirit of Mark's narrative!

the evangelical accounts, could only aggravate the doubt whether Christ in truth appeared separately to the women at all.

We proceed to examine the evangelical accounts of the appearances to the Disciples. And it must here strike us as remarkable that Matthew records no appearance in Jerusalem, and Luke no appearance in Galilee; similarly Mark, including the unauthentic appendix, and John in his first edition. In the last chapter of John, however, we have an account of a Galilean appearance, not to be identified with that narrated in Matthew, and yet hardly to be placed on either side of it. The two appearances are at different spots, to different persons, under different circumstances, and yet according to Matthew this appearance is plainly the first appearance of Jesus to the disciples in Galilee; according to John the one narrated by him must equally be the first appearance in Galilee, for it is the third appearance of Jesus to the disciples, of which the two former were in Jerusalem, xxi. 14. But as the appearances cannot both be the same, so they cannot each be the first appearance in Galilee.

The narrative of Matthew taken by itself leaves no room for any appearances to the disciples in Jerusalem at all. If the angels, if Jesus himself, told the women to direct the disciples to go into Galilee, with the addition—"there shall they see him"—"there shall they see me"—that almost implies that they should not see him in Jerusalem. That is what any person using the "ordinary language of common life," would mean by such a conjunction of expressions. And this implication is borne out by the subsequent narrative of Matthew, who says not a word of any appearance in Jerusalem. It is equally evident from his narrative that the appearance which he narrates is the first, and for all he says, and from the whole spirit of his representation, it might be the last, the first and only one therefore. In any case there is no room before it for the appearance narrated by John, chap. xxi. But as little is there room, as above shown, in John for the Galilean appearance of Matthew, before the one which he narrates. Thus the two gospels exhibit a discrepancy with reference to the appearance or appearances of Jesus in Galilee, which the Harmonist labours in vain to reconcile.

But as Matthew says nothing of any appearances to the disciples in Jerusalem, so Mark, Luke (and John in the first edition of his gospel) say nothing of any appearances in Galilee. But more, they seem to imply that there were appearances only in Jerusalem, and the two former, only on the day of the Resurrection, for they represent Jesus as taking leave of his disciples finally on that day, giving them his last instructions and commission, and being taken up into heaven. In the unauthentic conclusion of the second Gospel three Christophanies are recorded as having taken place on the day of the Resurrection—to Mary Magdalene, to two disciples going into the country, and to the Eleven, all apparently in Jerusalem, or the neighbourhood; and on the last of these the Ascension follows, taking the account as it stands, directly from the chamber where the disciples were assembled. John also records—omitting for the present the twenty-first chapter—three appearances, one to Mary Magdalene on the morning, and one to the ten apostles in the evening of the first day of the week, and one a week later to the Eleven. Luke also narrates three appearances, all on the day of the Resurrection; to the two disciples at Emmaus, to Peter, and to the Eleven and their companions; after which, apparently straightway, Jesus led them out to Bethany, and parted from them finally.

To press all discrepancies in the details of these various narratives would be an endless task, and as unprofitable as endless, for small objections admit of small answers, and both alike leave the root of the matter untouched. But there are two or three main points upon which any attempt to uphold the evangelical records in any detail, or to show their possible coherence as narratives, goes to pieces apparently. The one main point is, Galilee or Jerusalem as the scene of the Appearances; the other is, the time and place of the Ascension.

The obvious harmonistic answer to the first objection is; why not both Galilee and Jerusalem? And this answer was early given; for the chapter added to the fourth Gospel is in part at least a concession to the Galilean tradition: though we cannot suppose it a conscious attempt at an harmony. The incompatibility, however, of the appearance narrated in John xxi. with that narrated in Matt. xxviii. has already been shown; and so the Appendix to the fourth Gospel throws no light on the particular point here in question, but rather makes the difficulty more complicated. If the Angels and Jesus appeared to the women at and near the sepulchre and gave them the commission to the Apostles, as narrated circumstantially by Matthew, is it conceivable that Christ appeared two or three times to the disciples in Jerusalem, on the same day—to Peter, to the two at Emmaus, to the Eleven, assembled in the upper chamber at Jerusalem? Is it conceivable that the disciples were commanded to go into Galilee to meet and behold their risen Master; and that instead of obeying, they remained a week at least in Jerusalem, and during that time met and saw their risen Master several times ? And on what hypothesis are we to explain the fact that Matthew ignores all appearances to the disciples at Jerusalem, and at least Mark and Luke all appearances in Galilee, supposing there to have been appearances in both places, or in either place ?

The other point suggests even more inexplicable difficulties. The words put into the mouth of the risen Jesus by Matthew point naturally to the appearance which he relates being a final one, a leave-taking; and as such, we cannot doubt, this Evangelist regards it. But if the narratives of Mark and Luke are correct, Jesus had already parted from his disciples, after giving them their commission, in or near Jerusalem, on the day of his Resurrection. We are here indeed at the chief crux of the whole narratives singly and collectively, the Ascension. This—the greatest event in the history of the world, which, if possible, even more than the Resurrection itself might claim to determine our whole theory and practice—this event is not clearly related in any of the Gospels, but is so related by one of the Evangelists as to put him in hopeless contradiction with himself. It may be accepted as a highly probable result of criticism, that the author of the Acts of the Apostles, in its present form, is the same as the author of "the former treatise," which bears the name of Luke: and yet Luke makes the Ascension take place in his Gospel on the day of the Resurrection, and in the Acts of the Apostles narrates it with more circumstance, and places it forty days later. It cannot have taken place twice; and if it took place at all, it is hard to see how, with our notions of writing history, one and the same author could thus contradict himself on one and the same point.

It is strange indeed at first sight how little is made of

the stupendous event of the Ascension in the New Testament: it is strange, until we consider that for religion and practice the event had comparatively little significance. What had to be proved, was proved by the Resurrection; what had to be accomplished, was accomplished in the Resurrection; and the Ascension of Jesus had to his Resurrection much the same relation as the Roman General's Triumph up the Capitolium to his victory on the field. The Ascension did not put Jesus farther from his disciples, for he promised to be with them until the completion of the age (ἕως τῆς συντελείας τοῦ αἰῶνος, Matt. xxviii. 20): nor does it seem to have been necessary to their reception of the Holy Ghost, for according to the fourth Gospel at least, he imparted to them the Holy Ghost before his Ascension, and indeed on the day of his Resurrection (John xx. 22). Or was it indeed before his Ascension? Might it not seem from the narrative in the fourth Gospel that the Ascension took place between the appearance to Mary Magdalene in the morning, and the appearance to the Ten in the evening? (John xx. 17; cf. vii. 39.) Or, if we could harmonize the first and fourth Gospels, between the appearance to Mary Magdalene whom he forbids to touch him, because he is not yet ascended, and the appearance to the two Maries whom he allows to embrace his feet (Matt. xxviii. 9). Or are we here upon a trace of a primitive Christian consciousness which did not rigidly separate the Resurrection and the Ascension from one another? Do they together form one act, one event, in the glorification of Jesus? Matthew says nothing of an Ascension, and it might well be that according to his mode of conception the risen Jesus appeared straight out of heaven, as to Stephen, as to Paul: if we press the words in Mark the Ascension took place from a room, and can only have been a disappearance; nor is much more in Luke's Gospel: Paul* puts the appearance to himself after the Ascension in the same class as the appearances before the Ascension to others; and in his theology the elevation and entrance of Jesus into glory coincides with the Resurrection; Paul never says anything about the Ascension, and the supremacy and dominion of Christ is for Paul the immediate consequence of the Resurrection.†

What indeed if there was no visible Ascension? What if the strange scene, described in the first chapter of the Acts, but ignored by the Gospels, ignored by S. Paul and the rest of the New Testament writers, never separately appealed to in their preaching, though it might seem to signify so much—what if this scene should be rather poetical than scientific or historical truth? What if the Ascension, so easy of conception to men in the first century with their notions of the physical constitution of the heavens, so difficult to us with our notion of infinite space on all sides of us, and of our own endless motion through it—what if this should be a point where something of legend has mingled itself in the New Testament record? The first disciples were sure that Jesus was exalted, and set on the right hand of God; they might have seen his Ascension, as Elisha had seen the ascension of Elijah; is it impossible that their immediate followers, led by some such analogies, believed that the apostles must have seen the final departure of their Master? All the Evangelists narrate a final interview and leave-taking; what more natural, if the notion that Jesus had already gone to the

---

* Nothing can be more remarkable than S. Paul's omission of all mention of the Ascension, just where we might expect it—*e.g.*, Rom. viii. 34.

† Cf. Pfleiderer, "Der Paulinismus," p. 121.

Father, and made his appearance from heaven, was not vividly present to their consciousness, than that the first believers should have supposed a visible Ascension as a pendant to a last appearance? Those who have gone so far as to claim for the Gospels no immunity from the ordinary process of criticism, "realizing with the most strenuous endeavour every detail of their human characteristics," must find some difficulty in any longer imagining that the Apostles really saw Jesus ascend as described in the first chapter of the Acts (in contradiction to the third Gospel), and only there. It is a characteristic of popular consciousness to accumulate legendary and mythical details around a central figure, which has made a profound impression, and it would be strange if the figure of Jesus had been the only exception. It was not an exception, as we see from the apocryphal gospels. It is hardly less strange, once we have given up " the mechanical theory of inspiration" to maintain that this mythical and legendary accretion has left no trace, has made no deposit in the canonical books; that the process which is more and more apparent after their time, had not begun before they were written, before they received those additions and interpolations which every one recognizes in the four Gospels; or that having begun, it remained without influence upon these books, and was never a source of their narratives.*

* The belief about the Ascension of Jesus was no more uniform and unanimous in the early Church than any other belief. The *Patres Apostolici* say nothing of a *visible* Ascension, even in passages where it would aptly come in. The Latin Fathers lay most stress on the visible Ascension—a good deal of the materialism of popular Christianity is due to them. The Empress Helena built a church on the spot where the Ascension took place on the Mount of Olives: the place which the feet of Jesus had last touched

It is not necessary for the purpose of this Essay to enter here at length into the questions of the authenticity and the sources of the four Gospels. A discussion of these questions is indeed an indispensable preliminary to writing a Life of Jesus; but we are dealing here only in the main with an event which can hardly be said properly to belong to the life of Jesus, and with the appearances and secondary events connected with the Resurrection, of which accounts have been preserved to us in the concluding sections of the Gospels, which sections are confessed generally to be fragmentary, and in part unauthentic. Of the four Gospels, the third is the only

retained the prints, and could not be paved. That the Ascension was not only visible but bodily was an opinion supported by the arguments that Stephen had seen Jesus in heaven (Acts vii. 55 f.), that all shall see him at the last day (Acts i. 11; Matt. xxvi. 64; John xx. 37), and from the Eucharist, in which the Bread and Wine represent the true Flesh and Blood. Chrysostom argues that ἀναληφθείς (Acts i. 11), refers to flesh: even Origen did not teach that the Ascension wrought any further change on the body; and that the wounds were visible in the ascended body was an opinion shared by Epiphanius, Cyril of Alexandria, and Ambrose. Gregory of Nyssa, however, taught that the human nature had undergone a great change in the Ascension, and became perhaps even incorporeal. As in the case of the Resurrection so in the case of the Ascension, the earlier doctrine is that Christ ascended by the help of God: ἀνελήφθη εἰς οὐρανοὺς διὰ τῆς δυνάμεως τοῦ θεοῦ αὐτοῦ ἐπ' ὄψεσιν ἡμετέραις. Apost. Const. Later (Origen, Athanasius, Cyril of Jerusalem, Epiphanius), he ascended by his own proper might. Augustin furnishes a sort of harmony: "sublatus est Christus in manibus angelorum quando assumptus est in coelum; non quia si non portarent angeli, ruiturus erat, sed quia obsequebantur regi."—Some of the early heretics (Manichæans and Phantasiastæ) thought that Christ raised a fictitious body into heaven; others thought that he ascended as a pure Spirit. The Originistæ taught that the Body went on attenuating till it reached the Father—when none was left. (C. L. Müller, op. cit, §§ 24, 25, 26, 27.)

one in which the passages which refer to the Resurrection and subsequent appearances of Jesus do not show traces of interpolation and addition; and as if to destroy the unity of his evangelical record of the events subsequent to the Resurrection, Luke supplies a postscript in the first chapter of the Acts, which must either be false, or make the Gospel account false. The last twelve verses of Mark are confessedly unauthentic; the last chapter of John is an addition, hardly from the same hand which wrote the rest of the Gospel; in the first Gospel at least the passages referring to the watch at the sepulchre are probably a later insertion, and hardly formed part of the Gospel in its original form: and this Gospel in especial is open to suspicion as to details, from the legend-like peculiarities which have crept into it in connection with the death and burial. The most one-sided critic would not now deny the possibility of forming from the Gospels a picture of Jesus Christ, which should have some certain historical traits, and many possible and probable ones; but a great many critics, while differing one from another in their estimates of the nature of Christ and his place in the world's history, would agree that his figure has not escaped, even in the canonical books, legendary and mythical decoration, least of all in those parts of the Gospels which treat of the beginning and the end of his earthly existence. The impression made by the public ministry of Jesus, and by his personality upon his immediate followers, was a sound nucleus and starting-point for tradition; but his life up to his appearance in public after the arrest of John, was a field where fancy could unconsciously disport itself with less chance of contradiction, except from itself; and where the myth-making energy, which is a part of human nature just as much as the craving for systematization or coherency of knowledge, could find, if we may use a rough expression, fair game. The same may be said of the closing scenes of Jesus' earthly sojourn. They are confessedly supernatural and mysterious, or at least passing strange. If we held the theory of Inspiration we should expect that at such points as these the inspired writers would be specially guarded and directed; but this theory is practically abandoned as soon as the Gospels are seriously criticized; and on the theory of the natural origin of the records— such as is borne out by the two prefaces of Luke—it is just the supernatural or strange that would most easily afford a nucleus for legendary accretions. And these are just the parts which outside the Canon have received the legendary deposit most richly. The apocryphal writings of the New Testament relate many marvels of the childhood of Jesus, separated indeed from those preserved in the first and third Gospels by their vast inferiority both in point of morality and of good taste, but separated not in kind, since we have given up the theory of Inspiration, but only in degree. Perhaps the best and the worst samples of early Christian lore have survived, and the intervening members and species, the numerous sketches of the life of Jesus current in the primitive brotherhood (Luke i. 1), as is always the case in the struggle for existence, have dropped out, and are lost. The non-canonical Scriptures also contained narratives of the events subsequent to the Resurrection; and no absolutely hard-and-fast line can be drawn between the canonical and the non-canonical records. Thus "the Gospel of the Hebrews," the rival if not the original of our first Gospel, related the appearance of the risen Jesus to his brother James, which is not mentioned by any of our Gospels, though preserved by S. Paul. The Gospel of the Hebrews differs however from S. Paul, in representing the appearance to James as the first, not as the fourth. It is related* that with the sentry at the sepulchre was a servant of the high-priest, to whom the Lord gave the napkin (sindonem), and then went to James and appeared him; for James had made an oath that he would not eat to bread from the hour he had drunk the cup of the Lord until he should see him rising from the dead,—a vow which hardly admits of reconciliation with the state of mind of the Apostles at the death of their Master, as pourtrayed in the canonical Gospels. Jesus is then represented as blessing and breaking bread, and giving it to James, with the words: "My brother, eat thy bread, for the Son of Man is risen from them that sleep." Similarly the "Acts of Pilate," which now form part of the apocryphal Gospel of Nicodemus, were appealed to in the early Church in support of the miraculous events connected with the crucifixion, resurrection and ascension of Jesus; and Tertullian mentions expressly on this authority that Jesus spent forty days after his Resurrection with the Disciples in Galilee, and after giving them his last charges and instructions, was taken up to heaven on a cloud.† Tertullian, writing for Gentiles, appealed to evidence which he thought would be strong for them, and adds the words, "All this Pilate, whose conscience also drove him to become a Christian, wrote of Christ to the Emperor Tiberius." It need hardly be said that we have here a legend of a legend; and if this is so, who can affirm that nothing narrated of Pilate in the canonical Gospels is

* Hilgenfeld, "Nov. Test. extra canonem," IV. p. 17.
† Justin M. Apol. I. 35, 48. Tertullian, Apol. 21.

legendary? Nothing? It must be then because they are "canonical;" but what sort of assumption does such a statement presuppose? Certainly one which would amount to a claim for them to exemption from the ordinary processes of criticism. Those uncanonical writings, which give so much fuller details just in proportion, it might seem, as they are further removed from the events, were not all throughout deliberate falsifications and exaggerations; they are but more glaring instances, because for the most part less pure and primitive instances, of a process which, it can hardly be denied on critical ground, has already shown its influence in the canonical Gospels. The figures of Pilate and the Jews, of the Virgin Mary and the other women, of Nicodemus and Joseph of Arimathæa* are specially the subjects of decoration in these apocryphal writings: is the evangelical record unimpeachable touching those persons? These are the figures grouped, so to speak, by the Christian tradition round the sepulchre; and the certainty of the burial of Jesus and of the subsequent evacuation of the tomb, of which they are the witnesses, is one of the two principal sources of the belief in the Resurrection of Christ. Yet what is to be thought of the story in the first Gospel, which is enlarged upon in the Gospel of Nicodemus by all sorts of details and speeches, of the guard at the sepulchre? We might be tempted, in view of the silence of the other Evangelists, to think this story one of the last additions to the New Testament record,

---

* In the "Acta Pilati," c. 12 (Tischendorff's Evang. Apocryph. p. 293), Annas and Caiaphas put Joseph in prison; but he vanishes mysteriously, and is not to be found when they send to seek him; he is afterwards found at Arimathea (c. 15). He afterwards narrates to the priests his deliverance by Jesus in person.

and the motive for its addition would not be far to seek; it is a refutation of the very accusation ascribed to the Jews, that the body of Jesus had been stolen (xxviii. 13 ff.). The improbability of the story is large: the High Priests are represented as knowing a prophecy of Jesus which the Disciples are ignorant of, or have forgotten; and it is hardly a probable account of the psychological state of the grave and reverend Sanhedrim, who probably thought they had done God and his chosen people service in procuring the death of a religious impostor, that represents their precautions as due to a feeling of "uneasy guilt."* Neither is it very probable that the Sanhedrim would have been more busy on the feast-day than the Disciples, who "rested according to the commandment." Still more improbable is the story of the subsequent lie and bribery of the soldiers, whether we regard it from the point of view of the reality of what they are related to have seen, or from the more secure footing of Roman discipline. Moreover the women are represented as concerned at the difficulty of rolling away the stone, but as entertaining apparently no misgivings with respect to the military guard; so that the story is inconsistent with the rest of the narrative itself.

There are other details in the last chapters of the first Gospel, which reappear in the Apocryphal writings; and for this reason, as well as for their inner character, and the silence of the other Evangelists, these details have a suspicious and legendary air about them. Such are the miraculous phenomena that accompanied the death of Jesus. The fourth Gospel says nothing about them; the second and third report the darkness and the rending of

* Dr. Farrar.

the vail: the first adds an earthquake, rocks split, graves opened, appearances of the saints departed.* The apocryphal Gospel naturally goes further :† makes the Jews explain the darkness to Pilate as an ordinary eclipse of the sun (not very shrewdly, seeing that there was a Paschal full moon at the time); and knows the names of some of the Saints who appeared in the holy city, *e.g.*, Simeon,‡ "who received Jesus" [in the Temple]. These are just such events as a pagan would narrate as accompanying or presaging the death of one of his heroes.

> There is one within
> Recounts most horrid sights seen by the watch.
> A lioness hath whelpèd in the street,
> And graves have yawn'd and yielded up their dead;
> Fierce fiery warriors fought upon the clouds
> In ranks and squadrons, and right form of war,
> Which drizzled blood upon the Capitol:
> The voice of battle hurtled in the air,
> Horses did neigh, and dying men did groan;
> And ghosts did shriek and squeal about the streets.

> Jubeoque tremiscere montes
> Et mugire solum manesque exire sepulcris.§

And so "the singular and wholly isolated allusion of Matt. xxvii. 52-53," is too much even for the digestion which can assimilate the earthquake and the rending of the vail, and must be explained away; the earthquake "seemed to the imaginations of many to have disim-

---

* The Gospel of the Hebrews has: superliminare templi infinitæ magnitudinis fractum est atque divisum.

† "Evang. Nicod." XI. op. cit. p. 288.

‡ "Evang. Nicod." XVII. op. cit. p. 301. In the Anaphora Pilati Pilate gives the names of Abraham, Isaac, Jacob, the Twelve Patriarchs, Moses, and Job, and says he saw them himself. Tischendorff, Op. cit. p. 417.

§ Ovid, quoted in Keim, Jesu v. Nazara, III., 444, note 2.

prisoned the spirits of the dead, and to have filled the air with ghostly visitants, who after Christ had risen appeared to linger in the Holy City."* But it is a question of degrees. Matthew's is the only gospel which contains a record of the earthquake on the morning of the Resurrection; was this the agency which rolled away the stone; and was the angelic visitant who sat upon the stone, but a flash of lightning which, after Christ had risen, "appeared to linger" by the Holy Sepulchre?

Such an explanation reads to us like an ill-timed jest, yet such explanations have been attempted in all honour and seriousness chiefly by that Rationalistic school, which was for preserving the letter at the expense of the spirit, and assumed therefore that nothing was narrated that had not had something corresponding to it in fact, however unlike or arbitrary the fact and the record might be in essentials. So Matthew's angel was a flash of lightning; the angels in the other accounts were the grave-clothes, which the women, in their excitement at finding the tomb open and empty, mistook for shining apparitions; nay, the appearance to Mary Magdalene was not the risen Jesus, but, as she herself supposed, the gardener. It was a stroke of the same Rationalism to admit the reality of the appearances of Jesus, but to deny the reality of his death: the death was only apparent; the supposed corpse revived again (partly under the influence of the spices in which he was wrapped!) and left the tomb, the covering of which had been removed by the earthquake. It was very obvious to say that the glorious appearances of the risen Jesus were as unlike as possible to the

* Farrar, "Life of Christ," II. p. 419.

comings and goings of a feeble convalescent, or of an invalid, who shortly sank again under the hardships which he had sustained; it was very obvious that such a mere convalescence could never have restored and transfigured the faith of the Disciples, as, it is generally admitted, their faith was transfigured, after the Crucifixion. This Rationalism is to us nowadays but as a clumsy blunder; yet we must beware of falling into as clumsy a misapprehension of its meaning and intention.* It was honestly brought forward in the interest of Christianity and truth; it was an attempt in its day to satisfy at once reason and faith; it was the first most obvious and perhaps natural answer to the dilemma which science opposed to the biblical records: either Jesus was not really dead or he did not rise again. It was an attempt to justify the biblical records at the bar of Criticism, by such methods of apology as obtained in the last century, and the early part of this.

The attempt failed, and has to be made again; and now the word which by some is made to do duty for every other hypothesis, is the word "fragmentary." As the apologetic Rationalism of the eighteenth century sacrificed, so to speak, the supernatural facts in order to retain the truth of the narratives, so the rationalistic Christianity now in vogue, sacrifices the narratives—not merely their inspiration, but even their fulness and exhaustiveness from a human and historical point of view—in order to retain the supernatural facts. But does our Apology satisfy even the more modest criticism by this procedure? Can everything be explained by supposing the records fragmentary, by the implied supposition that were they

* As, for example, by Herder and Schleiermacher. Keim, III. 574.

complete, filled in, sufficiently supplemented, there would be found in them nothing self-contradictory, nothing legend-like, myth-like? There is one sort of contradictions indeed from which the Apologist may even derive support for his opinions, viz., that which concerns the nature of the risen body of Jesus, to which attributes are ascribed inconsistent with the nature of material bodies as we know them, and indeed inconsistent with the notion of a spiritual body, as many would conceive it. For to an Apologist who starts from a self-contradiction, viz., an absolute personality, contradictions of that sort may only seem so many confirmations and protections of the truth that the Resurrection was neither a mere coming back to life, nor the belief in it the result of mere visions. This is one of the points where we see ultimate metaphysical principles playing their part in moulding our views of facts, and learn how impossible it is to examine an alleged phenomenon apart from metaphysical presuppositions. But not to press this consideration, does the admitted fact that the records are fragmentary account for all? Does it account for the solitary and suspicious details in Matthew, already treated of? Does it account for such discrepancies as exist between the Christophanies in Galilee and in Jerusalem? or for the two representations of the Ascension, as given even by one author? Does it account for the words put into Jesus' mouth in these interviews? Is it conceivable, merely upon the basis of the "fragmentary" hypothesis, that Jesus gave four separate commissions to the Apostles, such as related in Matt. xxviii. 18 ff.; Mark xvi. 15 ff.; Luke xxiv. 46 ff.; John xx. 20 ff.? To which might be added a fifth, Acts i. 7, 8. And if these are all reproductions of one final charge, are they not more than fragmentary, have they not received additions, have they not received special terms and bearings, in accordance with later traditions or the views of the writers? Is it in any case conceivable that Jesus gave the Apostles express command to preach to all nations, and that long afterwards they were still debating whether or not the mission to the Gentiles was to be recognized? Is it conceivable that Jesus gave his Apostles a Trinitarian formula for Baptism, and that they never used it?

No; it is not possible to explain the relations of the records to each other in their present form, merely with the aid of the principle that they are fragmentary. There is after all some boundary to be set to the "discrepancies" of fragments, if they are to be admitted as historical evidence at all. And the fragments now in question are not merely contradictory; they show the action of a later consciousness, of ideas and disputes subsequent to the events which they narrate, they offer points of contact with writings outside the Canon, which are overloaded with legendary and mythical traits, and it is natural to ascribe similar effects to similar causes. But once admit that there are mythical and legendary traits in the evangelical accounts of the Resurrection, and what a flood of light is thrown upon the difficulties, the discrepancies and the similarities, of the various narratives! Why, they are then naturally just what we should expect in narratives thrown out by the unconscious process of the common mind of a community around the figure which is the object of its admiration and enthusiasm. Every nation, every religion has surrounded its heroes with a mythical halo, and enhanced their lives and deaths with a glory that is a witness indeed to the profound impression produced by the living men, but cannot be taken as accurately representative of fact. It would be strange indeed if the Christian community had been, by a miracle, absolved from this natural and unconscious impulse. It would be nearly as strange if the creative impulse had respected writings, which were indebted to the ordinary sources of their time for their narratives; writings which were not mechanically inspired, but as we are now agreed produced simply by natural processes: writings which only became canonical in progress of time, of a time which was itself constantly carrying on the unconscious work of superhumanizing, if we may coin the term, the Person of Jesus, and decided its Canon by considerations of the universal reception, antiquity, and probable authenticity of the writings in question, in short, by the only critical canons present to its consciousness.

And so indeed it comes to pass that the more intelligent or less preoccupied Apologists admit that the mythopœic and poetical imagination had already been at work before the Gospels were put together, and has had more or less influence upon their present form. And they know indeed how to convert the admission into an argument in favour of the chief matter which they have at heart; they sacrifice the form of the narrative that they may preserve the contents; they say, the details of the Resurrection are uncertain, and we cannot tell whether or not this or that story is true; but the uncertainty of the record only brings out more conspicuously the certainty of the fact. The Resurrection of Jesus, as Keim puts it, has, as a general fact, the strongest possible testimony in the New Testament, but the particular events connected with it, shrouded in contradictions and legendary lore, are the least to be trusted of anything in the whole region of the historical sources, even including the history of the childhood.* And from this point of view the argument must start not from the Gospels, which profess to give more or less detailed accounts, but from the witness of S. Paul; in other words the chief "moment" in the proof turns not on the empty grave, but on the Christophanies.

That S. Paul believed that, in some sense or other, Jesus rose on the third day from the dead† is a fact which admits of no question. He mentions the burial but not the empty grave; and the grounds of his belief in the Resurrection were apparently twofold: the appearance of Jesus Christ to him, which was the immediate cause of his conversion, and the five appearances to the first Disciples, of which he must have had oral testimony either before or after, or both before and after, his own conversion. The argument runs as follows:— The

---

* " Die Auferstehung Jesu im Allgemeinen gehört zum Bezeugtesten des N. T. die einzelnen Thatsachen aber, in Widersprüchen und Saghaftigkeiten schimmernd, sind noch über die Kindheitsgeschichte hinaus das Schlechtbezeugteste im ganzen Quellengebiete."—*Keim, Jesu v. Nazara*, III. 528.

With which the extreme statements of Strauss and Westcott may be compared:—" Selten ist ein unglaubliches Factum schlechter bezeugt, niemals ein schlechtbezeugtes an sich unglaublicher gewesen."—*Der alte und der neue Glaube*, p. 72.

"Taking all the evidence together, it is not too much to say that there is no single historic incident better or more variously supported than the Resurrection of Christ."—*Gospel of the Resurrection*, p. 126.

But Mr. Alger, who combines a personal belief orthodox on this point with a degree of critical acumen and integrity truly admirable, says:—" An unprejudiced mind competently taught and trained for the inquiry, but whose attitude towards the declared fact is that of distrust—a mind which will admit nothing but what is conclusively proved—cannot be driven from its position by all the extant material of evidence."—*Future Life*, p. 370.

† 1 Cor. xv.

conversion of Paul presupposes the faith of the earlier Christians, the faith of the earlier Christians presupposes the Resurrection; the Resurrection can alone adequately account for the visions which Paul narrates. His narrative was written probably in 58 A.D., but his conversion took place perhaps twenty years before,* that is to say about four years after the death of Jesus. We are here at last apparently upon *terra firma,* and have come to the test of the principles from which we set out. We have seen that the primitive Apostles during the lifetime of Jesus already believed on him, they believed that he was the Messias, the Son of God; and so it was plain that in their case it was not strictly correct to say that the doctrine flowed from the event, at least that the doctrine of Christ's Divinity flowed from the event of his Resurrection, as it is represented to do for us. But the case of Paul is different, and more like our own. Paul's belief that Jesus was the Messias was the result of his belief in the Resurrection; his belief in the Resurrection was the result of his vision; here is the doctrine apparently flowing from the fact; and the task for us is to determine the certainty and nature of the fact.

The fact that is here certain is the vision of Paul; and this certainty forms the point of departure for a construction, whether in an apologetic or in a critical sense. But the bare fact proves nothing, we must determine the nature of the fact, we must have an explanation, or *quasi*-explanation of the fact. One explanation is to say; Paul had a vision of the risen Jesus, because Jesus had in truth risen, and now willed to convince Paul of the fact of the Resurrection. But this assumes as proved

* Renan, "Les Apôtres," p. 163.

what is the very fact in question. Given the fact of the Resurrection, it is not difficult to explain the vision of Paul. But the fact of the Resurrection is the fact ultimately in debate; and the problem is, Given the vision of Paul, and the visions enumerated by Paul, is the fact of the Resurrection the only explanation of them?

Two broad facts may be taken as certain; that Paul and the other Apostles had certain visions, and that in consequence of these visions they believed that Jesus had risen from the dead. The Disciples, given the visions, had no other explanation of them but the fact of the Resurrection, for they brought the phenomena newly given, viz., the visions, into connection with a mass of doctrine in their minds already, and a readjustment took place in harmony with their general modes of conception and systematization of conceptions. Were those general modes of systematization and conception the same as ours? If not, were they truer than ours?

How would a Jew of the age of the Apostles have explained the occurrence of a vision? Would he have doubted of its objective reality? Would he have doubted of its supernatural origin? Would he have sought, as far as possible, to explain it from natural causes, before having recourse to the supposition of its heavenly origin? And what is specially to the point, would the Apostles have done so? Would S. Paul have done so?

We started by coming to a clear understanding of what was involved in the acceptance or rejection of the Resurrection of Jesus as an objective historical event: we find that the question of its objective reality reduces itself to the question, what explanation shall be sought and given of the visions of S. Paul and the Apostles? The conditions for the explanation of these visions are

its Evidence and Explanation. 69

the same as the conditions for the acceptance or rejection of the Resurrection as a real historical event. But conditions for the explanation of the visions must be presupposed in our case, for there were such conditions given *à priori* in the case of the Apostles: in short the explanation of the visions must be proved from and according to an already existing "view of the whole universe, of all being and of all life, of man and of the world, and of God." S. Paul and the Apostles had such a view; and they explained their visions in harmony with it; to speak more correctly, they did not hesitate or debate over the nature of the appearances, or their significance —the Lord is risen and hath appeared unto Simon, was the immediate and intuitional form of what argumentatively must run, The Lord is risen FOR he hath appeared unto Simon. It was their instinct, it was in harmony with their conscious and unconscious modes of thought, to assign a supernatural origin and cause to their visions: was their more or less unconscious explanation of the visions correct? Is it the one which we give, or can accept?

We are in the presence of two bodies of doctrine, of two orders of ideas, of two sets of presuppositions: the one, the uncritical unscientific mode of thought of a Jew in the first century, familiar with the notion of miracles, of supernatural interventions in the natural course of things, of heavenly warnings through dreams, and angels, of theophanies, and revelations: and this order of ideas has come down to us, loosened and modified in many respects by the gradual growth of another order of ideas, and gradually narrowed in its application and confined to one set or series of historical events, which in consequence have obtained the name of sacred history.

We have on the other hand a different order of ideas, we hold a set of different presuppositions, which goes by the name of the critical, the scientific mode of thought. Such thought finds no place in the systematization of knowledge for real miracles, for objective interventions of the supernatural in the natural course of events; but embodies and applies, so far as may be, the principle that all events are natural, and to be explained by natural laws and causes; that the continuity of phenomena is unbroken, and that consequently the explanation of any given phenomenon is to be found in its natural antecedents. Accordingly, where an explanation seems insufficient, we are not at once to have recourse to a supernatural factor as the special agent in the case, but either to trust to a review of the case in question and increased knowledge of natural circumstances and conditions, to furnish us with a natural explanation; or to repose in the conviction that if such increased knowledge were forthcoming in the given case, a natural explanation would be possible.

This mode of thought finds no place for miracles in its system, but it finds a place for the belief in miracles; the supernatural can be no part of nature, but a particular belief about the supernatural may be a purely natural product, a phenomenon to be explained from its antecedents, as much as any phenomenon can be explained. Philosophic criticism undertakes the attempt, not to explain a Christophany, but to explain how what it regards as a vision could be taken for a Christophany, nay more, must have been so taken.

That mode of thought which we may here call critical philosophy* has two apparent advantages over the mode

* Philosophy, really deserving the name, is always essentially critical, *i.e.* neither dogmatic on the one hand, nor sceptical on the

of thought previously described, and which may be called the supernaturalistic. The one advantage arises from a consideration of the general question of knowledge and its systematization; the other arises from a consideration of the historical relations between the two modes of thought. For the first: upon the presuppositions and maxims of criticism our knowledge in general rests; and it may easily be shown that only upon this basis can scientific inquiry, can observation and experiment, can history proceed. For purposes of inquiry and generalization it is necessary to presuppose that the course of nature and the course of history are not liable to interference *ab extra*, that their courses are respectively uniform, according to immanent laws, which it is the object of our investigation to discover. This being so, there is a *prima facie* case against any explanation of historical events, which involves a breach in the continuity of history, which separates one field of historical events, or one single historical event, from others, and still calls it history. For the second: two conclusions are to be drawn from the history of thought; the one, that the two sets of presuppositions have not always held the same relation to each other, but have for centuries been in a state of mutual hostility, the gradual course and outcome of which have been marked by a constant transference of territory from the supernaturalistic tradition to the dominion of critical philosophy: the other conclusion is,

<hr>

other; and in so far "critical philosophy" is a tautology. But so much talk and writing goes by the name of criticism, without being philosophic, or by the name of philosophy, without being critical, that it is not undesirable to keep before our minds the ideal of the truly philosophic temper, so long as it is liable to be confounded with bare appeals to the individual's reason and experience or to the more specious tribunal of hereditary catholic consent.

that every advance in natural knowledge, taking the term in the widest sense, has been made in practical, though not by any means in conscious, conformity to the critical presuppositions of knowledge, which may be most briefly stated as the principle, that the unknown resembles the known; with less ambiguity, that the events which have happened are to be understood by the light of the events which do happen, else they cannot be understood at all.*

Thus the problem for criticism in the present instance is: Given the visions of Paul and of the first disciples, to explain them, without the supposition of a special supernatural cause for the phenomena. And the materials which criticism has at its disposal are first, the general knowledge and principles which it would apply if the visions in question were phenomena of to-day or to-morrow; and secondly, the special knowledge of the circumstances and antecedents of the persons who had the particular visions in question. How far is it possible to account for these visions from a consideration of the natural conditions, external and general, internal and special, of the manifestations? If these conditions are such that a vision was possible under them, then criticism may claim to have made good its *prima facie* case, and a resort to transcendental causality may be pronounced out of place.

In attempting to explain the vision of S. Paul which brought about his conversion as a product of natural

---

* For a confirmation of the main position in this Essay, stated in more technical language than has been here attempted, I may refer to a pamphlet, "The Presuppositions of Critical History," by F. H. Bradley, Oxford, 1874, from which I might have derived considerable assistance had it fallen into my hands before the first chapter of this Essay was written, and the main line of argument—the relation between Fact and Doctrine—determined.

causes, we have to take into account the factors which would be appealed to as furnishing the explanation of a vision in any case. Is it conceivable, is it to be accounted for and pronounced even rational, that S. Paul should have had such a vision as he had, if it was only a natural vision? The factors from which an answer in the affirmative may be deduced can only be the general presuppositions (themselves generalizations of a large experience) which underlie the explanation of any alleged vision, and the special circumstances of S. Paul: and it should be conceded that not until we have exhausted the possibilities of these factors can we with any good reason have recourse to a transcendental causality to account for the given phenomenon. There is no question whether or not S. Paul ascribed his vision to such causality; the question is whether we are justified in so doing.

The psychological rationale of visions is something like this: Persons of a nervous temperament in moments of excitement are liable to have visual and other sensations, which, unless they are scientifically informed, they do not distinguish from perfectly normal sensations arising from external impressions, although in the case of visions the sensation is the immediate product of their own brain and nervous system. The contents of a vision generally reproduce former sensorial impressions, or, in other words, represent an object which the visionary has at some former time seen in a normal state of his organization; but a vision may also have contents which have never constituted a single sensorial state, which have never been present to the senses as an object before, the vision not being excited by an external object, but being a new form constructed " by a process which, if it had been carried on *consciously*, we should have called

Imagination."* It is very important here to notice, first, that sensorial states, or sensations, may be excited, not merely by external objects, but by ideas: in physiological language, that modifications of the sensorium, or cerebellum, may be produced not merely by changes in the nerves which communicate with the external periphery of the body, and so with the world outside, but by changes in the nerves which communicate with the cerebrum, or upper brain, which attains its maximum relative development in man, and is the specialized organ of thought. And it is to be remembered, secondly, that for those ignorant of the possible origin of their visions, the illusion has all the force of reality, and there is indeed no subjective criterion by which to distinguish sensations, which in themselves are essentially alike, and only differ in the sources whence they arise in the centre of sensibility. "Sensations of various kinds are distinctly felt by persons who are not only wide awake, but are entirely trustworthy in all other matters, though self deceived as to the reality of the objective sources of their sensations."†

Now if S. Paul had had a vision, as there was no such thing as a science of "Mental Physiology" in his day, he would certainly not have ascribed his sensations to "unconscious cerebration," or to the activity of his own brain and nervous system; he would not have looked for its causes among his ideas and his feelings. Certainly he was perfectly able to distinguish between a "heavenly vision" and an earthly appearance, but it could never enter into his thought to suspect the reality of the former,

---

* Carpenter: "Mental Physiology," § 103.
† Carpenter, op. cit. § 104.

its externality and independence; he would, if anything, have thought of it as more real than the things of sense, above and beyond them, and only matter of divine unveiling.

For how must we represent to ourselves the contents of S. Paul's vision? What was it that he saw? How did the dead and risen Christ appear to S. Paul, and with what body did he come?* S. Paul himself might call us "fools" for asking such a question, the answer to which was so obvious. Are there not celestial bodies and bodies terrestrial, differing from one another in glory? So also is the resurrection of the dead. It was not a glorious earthly body which S. Paul beheld, for flesh and blood cannot inherit the kingdom of God; it was a glorious celestial body, it was the spiritual body, it was the second man, the Lord from heaven. It was not Christ in his earthly body, the flesh and blood which he had taken of a woman, and which like all flesh and blood was corruptible, and could not inherit incorruption; it was Christ in the glory which he had in the beginning, before he was formed in fashion as a man, in a vile body;† it was the glory which was restored to him by the Father, the glory to which he had been restored in his Resurrection.

That this glorious body was immaterial would be too much to assert; the absolute mutual exclusiveness of the ideas of spirit and matter is a development of metaphysics in modern times which has little or no parallel justification in antiquity, least of all, in Christian antiquity, and which is even still a dichotomy that only the very fewest thinkers can carry through and apply consis-

---

* 1 Cor. xv. 35 ff.   † Phil. ii. 6 ff. iii. 21.

tently.* To them such an expression as "a spiritual body" may seem very like a *contradictio in adjecto*; but it was not so to S. Paul's mind, it is not so to the bulk of Christians now, whose idea of spirit is still the idea of something essentially material, even if they dilute it away to an invisible and imperceptible æther.† As S. Paul was necessarily in the dark on the subject of the æther rings out of which some modern physicists say the resurrection body is to be composed, he could not think of it as so invisible and so impalpable as it is now represented to be: but he thought of it naturally as composed of celestial matter, of the matter which belonged to the upper regions of light and æther,‡ regions which were heavenly indeed, yet not essentially impervious even to the earthly body (2 Cor. xii. 2), and whose matter therefore might very well become on occasion perceptible to the human eye.

It was therefore no difficulty to S. Paul that he had not seen Jesus on earth: he was indeed in his own opinion the least of the Apostles, unworthy to be called an Apostle, not, however, because he lacked the primitive qualification of having companied with the others all the time that Jesus went in and out among them, beginning from the baptism of John (Acts i. 21 f.), but because he had persecuted the Church. In other respects indeed he could boast of the genuineness of his Apostolate, as evidenced by the success of his preaching (2 Cor. ix. 1, 2),

---

* We must perhaps except Aristotle, with his criticism of the Platonic Idea as a mere reproduction of the sensible world; and his own theory of the highest reality in the Universe as an act of pure thought: νόησις νοήσεως.

† Cf. "The Unseen Universe."

‡ δι' ἠέρος αἰθέρ' ἵκανεν. Il. xiv. 288.

by the signs and wonders which accompanied it (Rom. xv. 19), by his self-devotion and martyr-like endurance on account of it (2 Cor. xi. 23 ff.), by the visions vouchsafed to him (2 Cor. xii. 1), above all by the crowning miracle and mercy of his conversion. He was not indeed appointed like Matthias, by human instrumentality, but by the direct interposition of God (1 Cor. i. 1 ; 2 Cor. i. 1), and he recognized no superiority in the primitive Apostles in Jerusalem (2 Cor. xii. 11 ; also xi. 6); he needed no letters of recommendation from them (2 Cor. iii. 1, 2), and he did not hesitate upon occasion to withstand the chief of them to the face (Gal. ii. 11). Nay, it might almost seem to have been in Paul's eyes a disadvantage or a superfluity to have been a companion of the living Jesus (2 Cor. v. 16, 17), and the whole of Paul's Gospel was summed up and comprehended, not in the teaching, not in the miracles of healing, of the Messias, but in his shameful death and glorious resurrection. This was the Jesus whom Paul knew and preached; death with him in his Crucifixion, and life with him in his Resurrection, was the sum and substance of Paul's Gospel: the law of the spirit of life which wrought deliverance from the law of sin and death (Rom. viii. 2) : and if anyone, an angel of God himself, preached any other Gospel, save Jesus Christ crucified, this word of the Cross, this scandal to Jews and folly to Gentiles, yet word of divine power and wisdom, let him (said S. Paul) be accursed.

Whence this all-absorbing importance of the death and resurrection of Christ in S. Paul's Gospel ? What is the significance of these facts to him ? What is this "other Gospel" and "other Jesus" against which he protests so vehemently ?* What is the meaning of the fact that he

* Gal. i. 7, 8 ; 2 Cor. xi. 4.

who before his conversion was breathing out threatenings and slaughter against the Church in Jerusalem, seems after his conversion to be breathing out anathemas against members and emissaries of that same community?

That there was a substantial difference between the teaching of S. Paul and the teaching of the original apostolic community, is a conclusion which lies clearly before us in the New Testament itself, when once the scales of an abstract dogmatism have fallen from our eyes. This conclusion is so probable in itself, when we consider the circumstances of the Apostolic college and of the new convert; and throws such a flood of light upon primitive Christianity, that if there are people who still cannot recognize it, they must be outside the pale of those who are willing or anxious to apply to the origin of Christianity, with a view to elucidating at least the human instrumentality by which it was developed in its cradle, the ordinary canons and presuppositions of critical history. That after the conversion of S. Paul there were two main parties in Christendom who gave different accounts of the fundamental principle of their religion, that the heads of these two parties were respectively the primitive Apostles in Jerusalem and S. Paul, now at Antioch, now at Ephesus, now at Corinth, now in prison in Rome, is a view of the facts of early Christianity not seriously clouded by the harmonistic attempts of the author of the Acts of the Apostles, and set in the light of day by S. Paul's own authentic writings, to say nothing of the confirmation lent to the case by the pseudo-Clementine Homilies. That this dispute was not one of a simply personal character, between the authority of Paul and of Peter and the other pillars of the Church, but involved doctrinal differences, is no less evident. It is his Gospel, the Gospel of Christ, the word of the Cross, for which S. Paul is anxious, and he only asserts his personal authority as a support of the doctrine which he taught. That doctrine was simply that Jesus Christ was an end to the law, at once its fulfilment and its abolition. The Law once abolished, there could no longer be any wall of partition between Jew and Gentile; nor could it be any longer necessary for Jews to observe the law, much less for Gentile converts to Christianity to undertake the onerous obligations of an intercalary and now exploded system of positive and negative commands. This catholic emancipation was the glorious liberty of the children of God. (cp. Gal. v.)

But such Antinomianism the brethren in Jerusalem could not stomach or comprehend; probably they saw only its negative side, and like every new principle which has not made good its position as a matter of fact and of conduct, this liberty was a stumbling-block to them, seemed to open the door to arbitrary licence, and to be an excuse for sin. To them also Christ was the fulfilment of the law, but not its abolition; his followers were still to strive for righteousness by works of the law, the law was still binding upon them. These simple men of Galilee had been with Jesus during his lifetime, had been witnesses of his deeds and recipients of his word, and had felt the power of his immediate presence, so that they too out of weakness were made strong: but they had looked for the death of the Messias as little as any Jews of their days; they were unprepared for it when it came; and they never grasped its full significance, even after they were assured that Jesus was risen from the dead. To them the death of the Messias was a stumbling-block removed by his Resurrection, but it was a stumbling-block, rather than the necessary means of his glorification and the realization of his kingdom: and hence the Resurrection was in their preaching of first prominence, for it restored to them their confidence in the lost Master. They could now work and wait, with patience and assurance, for his speedy reappearance to establish the kingdom, wherein they were to sit on twelve thrones judging the twelve tribes of Israel. Meanwhile, like John Baptist, they preached repentance and forgiveness of sins, as the necessary preliminaries and qualifications for a part in the coming kingdom. Into the name of Jesus they baptized those who joined them, and they may well have regarded his death, in the light of the legal sacrifices, as propitiatory; but the death of the Messias was in itself like the death of the prophets of old the work of the people and their rulers, an untoward generation, and in so far accidental, so to speak, not essential in the divine scheme of salvation. Not indeed as if the Crucifixion of the Messias had happened without the determinate counsel and foreknowledge of God, for none of the trials of his servants, none of the perversity of those who hardened their hearts against him, was independent of his providential guidance; but it was not the *sine qua non* of the realization of the Messianic hope. The Messias, like his ancient type Moses, might have supposed that his brethren would have understood how that God by his hand would deliver them; but they understood not, and so became the murderers of the Just One. Yet that same Jesus whom the House of Israel had crucified, God had made both Lord and Christ, the proof of which was his Resurrection, whereof the Apostles were witnesses.

To a Jew indeed the death of Jesus upon the cross was, as it were, the divine judgment upon him as an impostor, as a blasphemer. But if God had afterwards raised him from the dead, that apparent judgment was cancelled, and converted into a divine ratification of his claims and promises. "If he be the Son of God, let him descend from the cross." So the assertion of the Resurrection of Jesus by his Apostles might well prick those that heard it in their hearts, and rouse consternation among their rulers: for if the assertion were true, they had indeed been guilty of fighting against God, and might expect a divine judgment upon their heads. What wonder if they attempted to silence the Apostles? What wonder if, since they could not deny the possibility of the asserted fact, they should spread a report among the people that his disciples had come by night and stolen the body of the dead impostor?

Among those who in their zeal carried opposition to the new community, founded within three or four years of the death of Jesus on the faith in his Resurrection, even to the pitch of violent persecution, was one destined subsequently to spread that very faith among the Heathen. An Hellenic Jew of the tribe of Benjamin, and at the same time perhaps a Roman citizen, a Pharisee and the son of Pharisees,* of much learning, trained at the feet of Gamaliel (the grandson of the illustrious Hillel), the young man Saul was of a very different type to the unlearned and ignorant leaders of the new movement; but he was already the same man who should one day be the Apostle of Christianity to the Gentiles. His conversion changed the contents of his mind, the objects

---

* "Perhaps only in a spiritual sense."—Hilgenfeld.

of his enthusiasm, the direction of his zeal, but it was not his conversion that first gave him zeal, enthusiasm, affection, or the dialectical and logical power which are characteristic of "the least of the Apostles." His conversion was indeed in the profoundest sense a moral change, a moral revolution, but hardly in the vulgar sense in which a drunkard is "converted," when he takes to platform preaching. Before his conversion S. Paul was, touching righteousness according to the Law, blameless (Phil. iii. 6), but the great moral change in him was the birth of a new moral principle, a new moral consciousness, a new moral freedom, the discovery of a new source whence he could satisfy his thirst for righteousness, the transit from the obedience of a servant to the obedience of a son, from bondage under a law divine but still external, to identification spiritually with a divine Person, who had died to the Law and was now alive unto God.

Such was S. Paul's Gospel, the revelation of Jesus Christ in him, the word of the Cross, the wisdom of God. He was resolved to know nothing but Jesus Christ, and Him crucified. For S. Paul the death of Christ was not something accidental; it was the essential principle of Christianity, the blood of the new Covenant, the power of God and the wisdom of God. The death of the Messias was the abolition of the Law, and as to S. Paul this death was part of the divine purpose and plan of salvation, the abolition of the Law must also be the divine purpose. The Law once abolished, room was made for a new principle of righteousness, Faith, since the old principle was annulled and superseded; and for a new life of Faith, by which the Christian died daily to sin, by his mystical union with the life of the crucified and risen Christ.

But that the death of the Messias involved the end of the Law, and of the pursuit of righteousness by works of the Law, was a principle which S. Paul may, nay we may say must, with his logical and dialectic mind, have seen before his conversion. Was it not the very perception of what was really involved in the assertion that the Crucified was nevertheless the Messias, that intensified the hostility of the zealot for the Law against the Disciples of Jesus? Saul, with his mind preoccupied by all the doctrines of a highly educated Pharisee of that day, regarding the Law as final and valid for all people, so that the Gentiles could only be partakers in the salvation in store for Israel by becoming proselytes, and subject to Israel's Law, is met by the assertion that the Messias, for whose near approach he, in accordance with the general expectation of the more religious part of the nation, was looking, was already come, and had been rejected and slain by the people and their rulers. At first he may have repelled the notion as monstrous and absurd; but he could not come into closer contact with the members of the new religious community, he could not speak with them, or witness their cheerful sufferings and even death on account of their belief, without at least acknowledging that they were honest and profoundly in earnest, and fully persuaded that they had seen their crucified Master risen from the dead. And thus, as the Pharisee Saul could not deem it a thing impossible that God should raise the dead, the possibility was given to him at least in thought, that what these men had said was true; that they had indeed seen their risen Master, and that he was in consequence, as they asserted, the Messias. But the further consequences involved in the last assertion could not remain, to Saul's energetic and dialectical mind, long undeveloped; and the perception of their ultimate issue, the abrogation of the Law, still to him a mere negation, could only increase the zeal of the lover of the Law against his antagonists. Yet how to meet their repeated assertion that they had seen the Lord after his Resurrection? Could Saul ascribe it to falsehood and deception, when he witnessed the honesty and devotion of the men who made the assertion? Could he fail to perceive that such ascription was an illogical assumption of the very matter in dispute?

Saul was in the attitude of mind, as far as thought is concerned formally, which we described in the first chapter; he had a body of doctrine in his mind, and in contact with this was now set a new fact, which refused to harmonize with the existing body of doctrine in his mind, and which he yet could not absolutely disprove. It was not credible, as was asserted, that the crucified Jesus was the Messias, as he would be if God had raised him from the dead; for in that case the Jewish nation had rejected its Saviour, and there was an end to the Law: and yet these men persisted in saying that they had seen him, that God had raised him from the dead. He could not believe them; yet he could not disprove what they said. For such a mind as S. Paul's this state was one of intellectual torture.

And already in his heart of hearts, in the fervent depth of his religious nature, had Saul not an inkling of the freedom and rapture which this new fact, if it were after all a fact, might carry as the positive side of what seemed to him so far perhaps but a mere negation? Is there any one that has ever had occasion, even on a small scale, with no such mighty nature as S. Paul's, than whom perhaps,

> A rarer spirit never
> Did steer humanity,—

but in his own degree, completely to alter his fundamental beliefs; who does not know how what he now holds for truth seemed to him once impossible, monstrous, perhaps impious and unholy; and yet seemed to draw him in spite of himself, so that he at once feared to face it, and feared to flee, and would fain have sought relief in some manual occupation, or bodily activity?

However this may be, it cannot surprise us that the very moment of Saul's greatest apparent hostility to the faith of Jesus should be the moment of his conversion. The dialectical process in his mind was (we may suppose) at its height, or even, it may be, carried through, and decided against the asserted fact, which his mind could not assimilate. Yet this decision, if formed, was but a hollow one, for Saul was not really in a position to deny the possibility of the disputed fact. The result of this energy of thought was an accession of the innermost religious excitement. Thus with a naturally highly strung nervous temperament now highly wrought upon, with the vegetative functions of his organization impaired perhaps by fasting or mental preoccupation, Saul was just in the state of mind and body to have such a vision as we have described above as the result of great mental activity; to be the subject of sensations arising not from an external object, but from internal ideas, produced in the sensorium not by the nerves that connect the cerebellum with the periphery of the body, but by the nerves which connect the central organ of sensation with the cerebrum, or organ of thought. Such a vision was not a reproduction of sensorial impressions formerly received—for Saul had never seen Jesus—but a construction of new forms by a process which, if it had been carried on consciously, we should have called Imagination: but which, for the subject who does not carry it on consciously, is indistinguishable from sensations produced by an external object.

What the *contents* of S. Paul's vision must have been, we have already seen as an inference from his own conception of the spiritual body. Whether the vision had an external occasion, whether the forms which his thought had been preparing, were precipitated so to speak by some natural event, a thunderstorm or what not, as might perhaps be inferred from the accounts in the Acts, though in part inconsistent with each other, is a secondary question, the answer to which does not much matter, whichever way it fall. There may have been a thunderstorm on the way to Damascus, and Saul may have been dazzled and struck to the ground by it; but it is not indispensable to the explanation of the vision, which may have had purely mental and bodily states as its sufficient cause. That the vision may have been joined with a revelation, that Saul may not merely have had visual sensations, but also audible sensations, is a supposition which lies well within the range of psychological probability. We have not indeed his own authority for making any positive statement on this head; but he must have asked himself many times why he was persecuting the men who had been with Jesus, and must already have felt deeply in his soul the goads which his own insight and the mental throes through which he had passed, prepared for him. He may therefore very well have heard a voice saying to him in the Hebrew tongue—" Saul, Saul, why persecutest thou me? It is hard for thee to kick against the pricks!"

In his philosophy Saul had only one explanation for his vision; it was the work of God, a direct divine interposition in his favour; it was the revelation of the Messias, of the crucified Messias. Saul had already (we suppose) developed in his own mind the significance and consequences of this fact, at least in the main outline; hitherto indeed these consequences had been negatived in his mind, but now in one moment they were turned into his most positive convictions. He already knew, we may suppose, from his disputes with the followers of Jesus, how little any of them really grasped the full significance of the facts which had been in dispute between himself and them, viz., the death and resurrection of the Son of God. Of the truth of those facts he was now convinced, but the new convert did not return to Jerusalem to learn from those who had known Jesus while yet on earth, the details of his life and teaching, nor did he confer with flesh and blood in Damascus, but retired into solitude there to develop in detail all the consequences of the two facts, which for him were the Alpha and Omega of the Gospel, the Death and the Resurrection of the Christ. And so it comes to pass that S. Paul, although he has left us but a few letters, which with one exception (Ep. to Romans) make no pretence at giving a resumé of his system, but arose out of special occasions, nevertheless stands before us in them as a theologian with a thorough and well articulated system, always the same and self-consistent, without change or development, if we except perhaps his eschatology.* Herein he seems at first to have shared the cruder expectations of a speedy return of the Messias,

---

* Cf. Reuss, "Geschichte der h. Schriften, N. T." 1860. 3te Ausg. § 63.

which played so important a *rôle* in Jewish Christianity; but to have laid more and more stress, as years went by, and still the Messias did not appear in the clouds for the day of the Lord, on the present spiritual union with Christ, and on the prospect of closer union with him immediately after death.

Not that S. Paul ever broke so completely with Judaism as that other New Testament author whom we associate with the name of S. John. Even in opposition to Judaism Paul was still a Jew, and could only refute Jewish orthodoxy, to use a technical expression, in its own categories; Sin and Sacrifice, Predestination and Fulfilment, Miracle, Prophecy, Allegory and Resurrection. Moving in this circle of ideas, with such physical and psychological knowledge or ignorance as was shared by educated men of his nation and time, there could occur to him one and only one explanation for his vision, which *we* may think of as the product of his own mind working upon a given fact—(the assertion that Jesus had been raised by God from the dead)—a mind eminently logical to follow out into all details a given premise, a mind intensely religious, and fervent for truth, in a body not at the best of times free from disorders, which may have been in part the cause and in part the effect of his mental temperament, and may be also taken into the reckoning as a factor in predisposing his mind to visions.

There is indeed even at first sight so much about the conversion of S. Paul which admits of being referred to natural causes, that a judicious Apologist may at times seem to pass too lightly over its evidential value and significance. Thus Dr. Westcott says*; "For us the

---

* When Dr. Westcott adds a note to the effect that "It is important to observe that on another occasion S. Paul notices the

appearance to S. Paul would certainly in itself fail to satisfy in some respects the conditions of historic reality—it might have been an internal revelation—but for him it was essentially objective and outward;" it took place indeed at a time "when the idea of the risen Christ was fully established," as the same writer says in another passage.* Yet still it remained a psychological problem, which even Baur declared insoluble. In the presence of two facts—first, Paul's own repeated assertion of the reality of the appearance, and second, the originality of his Christianity, its independence of all instruction from the Apostles, it was, said Reuss in 1860,† a mistake to see nothing in the affair but a thunderstorm and an overstrained imagination (Phantasie). Perhaps the door was here intentionally left open for some supernatural cause

doubt which he felt as to the objective character of the revelation which he received (2 Cor. xii. 1 ff.)," he seems to imply that "in the body" is equivalent with S. Paul to our term "objective," and "out of the body" to our term "subjective." This is a strange misconception. S. Paul is obviously speaking of his earthly body, and expresses a doubt whether or no when he was caught up to the third heaven, into Paradise, his body was left on earth or not. It would have been rather odd in a dialectician of S. Paul's calibre to appeal to a vision which he granted might be regarded as "subjective" in support of his apostolic dignity.—Op. cit. 112.

When the same writer, in the second passage referred to, speaks of the appearance "granted to St. Paul" as "different in kind" from the appearances to the first believers, it is sufficient to remark that S. Paul (who never speaks of the empty grave or of the Ascension as a separate phenomenon) justifies no such assertion, but rather shows by the juxta-position of his own and the other visions, that it never occurred to him to doubt that the appearance to him was generically the same as the appearances to the others before him, and only differed from them in being last.

* Op. cit. p. 158, note.
† Op. cit. p. 49.

short of "an absolute miracle of the old theological pattern;" but the writer proceeded: "On the other hand no healthy theology can rest in the notion of a mechanical transformation of a noble and great spirit *ab extra* (gezwungen), by which notion the true providential guidance of the whole work of salvation would rather be called in question." In the following year (1861) Dr. C. Holsten published his essay, "Die christusvision des Paulus und die genesis des paulinischen evangelium,"* in which he attempted to solve the problem in the interests of historical criticism, by a most careful analysis of the natural conditions general and special, internal and external, which may be assumed as antecedents of Paul's vision. The most original and fruitful idea in this analysis is perhaps the principle that from the Pauline Gospel as it lies before us in S. Paul's authentic writings, and from the intellectual and moral character of S. Paul therein exhibited at once in its opposition to Judaism and its own essentially Jewish form, is to be extracted the key to the problem of Paul's conversion. The present writer does not pretend to have improved this master-key, if it needed improvement; but borrowed and used with the discretion, even of an apprentice, it seems to fit the lock, and the secret to fly open; so that we can hardly escape the conclusion of a philosopher of our own, who has taught us a great respect for facts, when he says that the conversion of S. Paul " of all the miracles of the New Testament is the one which admits of the easiest explanation from natural causes."†

But this explanation presupposes the idea of the risen

---

* Now printed in his work, "Zum Evangelium des Paulus und des Petrus." Rostock, 1868.

† J. S. Mill: "Three Essays on Religion," p. 239, note.

Christ, presupposes the belief of the first Apostles, presupposes their vision, or visions, which S. Paul has enumerated as antecedent to his own; for was not that idea or that belief obviously not the cause but the product of those visions? Thus it might seem that the more successfully criticism extended its claim to the vision of S. Paul, the more completely it cuts itself off from the visions of S. Peter and the other primitive believers: given their belief, the vision of S. Paul may be fairly represented as a product of natural causes, of which this very belief of theirs is one; but whence their belief? Must not the visions of Peter and his companions seem wonderful and supernatural just in proportion as the vision of Paul is made out to be natural? And if so, whereto all this trouble to make out the natural causality of the Pauline vision, when it would be much simpler to ascribe all alike to divine interposition, to an objective-transcendental source?

The feeling expressed in the latter sentence is one shared by criticism, whose fundamental canon must ever be to follow the lines of nature in her dissection, and neither to part from each other things generically similar, nor to confound together things generically different. And so in the present instance having sought and found a plausible explanation for one given fact in its natural antecedents, it is not to be expected that criticism will so lightly abandon the effort to explain another fact, generically the same as the problem which she has solved approximately, or leave such a lump undigested in her knowledge, such a thorn, which to her too is as a messenger of Satan, rankling in her body.

Let us here again start from the given facts, so far as we can in outline restore them with any confidence. If there is anything certain it is that the Disciples of Jesus regarded him, that he regarded himself, as the expected Messias : but it is not less certain that their conception of the Messias and his destinies differed very widely from their Master's own consciousness of his mission and the means of its accomplishment, perhaps from the very first, without doubt towards the close of his career. Given the self-consciousness of his divine mission and the facts of his life, it is not surprising that Jesus should have grasped the spiritual idea of a suffering Messias, and once in possession of it have found support for it and authority in the Old Testament, foreign as was such an interpretation to the Jews of that time; and if so, he must have sought to bring home this spiritual idea to his Disciples : but it is still a question how far he expected his Death; much more, how far he had assimilated and harmonized this expectation or possibility with the inner conviction of his own Messianic dignity. If the case here were such as it is represented to be by the ordinary supernaturalistic theology, then the struggle in the soul of Jesus, of which a tradition has come to us in the *synoptic* account of the night in Gethsemane, and the last loud cry on the cross, as preserved by Matthew and Mark, are quite inexplicable, except as what in less solemn connection would be called acting; and that the fourth Evangelist felt this, more or less consciously, is shown by the turn which he has given to the scene in Gethsemane, which in his account has lost all sign of struggle in the all-knowing Son of God, who neither prays to his Father to suffer the cup to pass from him, nor betrays the slightest bodily agitation; and further in his omission, like Luke, of the "Eli, Eli, lama sabachthani; My God, my God, why hast Thou forsaken me!"

the last words of the dying Master recorded by the two earlier Evangelists, which throw light, so terrible yet human, into "the divine depth" of his sorrow. Infinitely more probable must it appear, on any theory which admits a discussion of probability into the matter at all, that even up to the last Jesus may have expected a divine interposition in his favour, and, when after all no such interposition took place, may have felt himself forsaken of God : though there is no one who would not wish to believe that the innocent sufferer regained his consciousness of perfect peace with God, as implied in the commendation of his spirit into his Father's hands, recorded by Luke, or even the self-assurance of the completion of his intended work as implied in the "It is finished" of S. John.

But whether or not Jesus foresaw his own death, and the necessity of it to the completion of his mission, it is perfectly certain that these profound ideas remained entirely dark and inexplicable to the Disciples: otherwise they could not have come to him on his way to Jerusalem with such crude and ill-timed requests, as they are represented to have done (Mark x. 35 ff.), nor could they have been so utterly unprepared for the event when it took place, or have so entirely lost heart and faith in their Master, as they apparently did. On the contrary his sufferings and death, which he had accurately foretold to them, would have been a fresh confirmation of his prophetic power and divine mission, and they would have waited in quiet assurance for his Resurrection on the third day which he had explicitly foretold them several times (Matt. xvi. 21 ; xvii. 9-23 ; xx. 19 ff. ; xxvi. 32 ff. ; cp. Mark x. 34 ; Luke xviii. 33 ; xxiv. 7). Could they have forgotten all this at his death, and have only thought of a robbery when they found the tomb empty (if they found it empty); have doubted the report of his Resurrection (Luke xxiv. 11), and been incredulous still even when they saw him (Matt. xxviii. 17)? If the Apostles little expected the death of their Master, still less did they expect his Resurrection; and he cannot have foretold it as he is represented to have done.

But it may be said, granted that the Disciples had no expectation of the return of their Master to life, then all the more improbable that the appearances to them were merely visions; one natural source of visions is cut off —expectancy.

Let us look a little closer at the circumstances and mental state of the Disciples, when the fatal event fell upon them, shattering apparently at once their faith in their Messias, and their hopes of a speedy restoration of the kingdom to Israel, and of a foremost rank in that kingdom for themselves.

On the arrest of Jesus these men, who for at least a good year, perhaps for longer, had been his chosen companions and confidants, who a few days before had been spectators and co-operators in his enthusiastic reception in Jerusalem as the royal prophet, were so unmanned by consternation and overcome by faithless fear that they all forsook him and fled. Whether they were at once all scattered to their homes in Galilee, as might seem not improbable, or remained, at least one or more of them, in Jerusalem, we can hardly decide with assurance. But wherever they might be, whether in the scenes so intimately associated with their Master's presence in Galilee, or in the city, now the centre of their interest as the place of his violent death, it could not but be that a nobler mind should reassert itself in them, the panic of the moment once over. These men, unlearned and ignorant as they might be, must yet have had a strong chord of sympathy with their spiritual Master to have made them his friends at all. How this chord must now have vibrated, not merely under the stroke of his death, but under shame and contrition for their own cowardly conduct! And if any tidings came to them through the women, who followed Jesus to Calvary itself, of his last moments, of his sublime patience and trust in God to the last that he would deliver him, of his love to the last for those whom he left behind, how vastly must their shame and confusion have been increased! God had not delivered him, as it seemed; and they with their Jewish way of looking at material events, and seeing everywhere a direct divine judgment, had been tempted perhaps to regard the arrest and death of their Master as God's sentence upon him. But the instinct of their women had been other, and had shamed them at least in their desertion and flight: nay, they might recall teaching of the lost Master himself, in which he had sought to correct and enlarge similar partial views of the divine course and guidance of events (Luke xiii. 1 ff.); and as they remembered and mutually excited their remembrance of his person and his teaching, spite of their baffled hopes, spite of his dishonoured death, spite of their own shameful desertion and moral cowardice, they must have felt themselves in fault, they must have cleared him in their minds, and as their better consciousness reasserted itself, it was they, if anybody, who said, "Truly this man was the Son of God."

If there is any historical credibility in the Gospel narratives of the Resurrection at all, if they give us any materials for the reconstruction of events and characters, we may infer that no Apostle in the hours and days immediately following the catastrophe which revealed the thoughts of all hearts concerned in it, was so convulsed and overwhelmed by the experiences of the moment as Peter. Naturally enough; for none had stood so high or fallen so low. Peter had belonged to the inner circle of the friends of Jesus; Peter had been the recipient of special favour and reliance, and had ever been most forward in professions of belief and devotion. Of a hasty and enthusiastic yet vacillating temper (cp. Gal. ii. 11 ff.), Peter had perhaps been ready in the first moment that danger overtook his Master to stand by him and draw weapon in his defence; yet within a few hours perhaps none had so explicitly renounced all connection with Jesus. In none could the reaction be more sure and complete. Peter, in whom we may fairly see a mixture of strength and weakness, which gave him a certain originality, combined an ambitious self-assertion with an intelligence by no means so logical or powerful as Paul's. His nature was elevated by a genuine religious fervour, which had been developed and concentrated by the Master whom he had denied and lost. In such a nature, after such a collapse, must have arisen a psychological necessity for a restoration of self-respect, and of the sense of reconciliation with the departed Jesus, the assurance that Jesus had forgiven him. That this is no hypothesis taken out of the air is proved by a glance at the Christian tradition itself, which shows the instinctive feeling that some special intimation must have been received by Peter before he could have regained self-assurance or respect from his companions. (Mark xvi. 7; Luke xxiv. 34, cf. Luke xxiv. 12; John xx. 3 ff.; xxi. 15 ff.) And what in Paul was produced chiefly through the action of the dialectic of thought, and its influence on the centre of sensation, may have been produced in Peter by the dialectic of feeling, by the tempest of conflicting feelings, shame, self-reproach, love, which threatened to overwhelm him as once the waves on Galilee's lake, and above all the image of the Master in all his power and purity reasserting itself in his mind, till he felt that every man might be a liar, but not this man, not the Son of the Highest.

And then under circumstances of time and place, which have not been reported to us, Peter sees his Master again, and receives from him, doubtless, some sign, perhaps some words, of forgiveness and restoration. In what form he saw Jesus, whether as in the body or in a glorified shape, we cannot say; could we cross-question the Apostle as to the details of his vision, he might waive such items, as did Joan of Arc when cross-questioned as to the appearance of S. Michael, whom she frequently saw. The outlines of a vision are not always hard and fast; and if the visionary tries to fix them, they melt often like cloud before his eyes : that is proof to him, not of the unreality but of the supernatural character of what he sees ; and all the more so, if the vision is accompanied by words, even by dialogue, as was the fact in the case of Joan of Arc. In the latter case, an uneducated peasant girl, who could not write her name, who had no mental equivalent for such an abstract idea as the Church, when asked did she acknowledge its authority; who, with the Council of Basel sitting at the time, did not know what a Church Council meant, had yet seen and conversed with Angel and Archangel, and distinguished them by their voices many times : and she was in all other respects of the strongest and soberest practical understanding, and carried out the directions which she received from above in a way which, humanly speaking, was a series of strokes of genius. And are we to be told that what, in the hour of need, in the case of a French peasant girl in the fifteenth century, was produced, so far as we can see, by a deeply religious temperament coupled to patriotic and loyal ideas, could not have been produced in a Galilean peasant of the first century by similar causes of greater intensity? Peter also had loyal and patriotic ideas, and magnificent expectations for his Master, for his nation, for himself, and above and beyond this, had the pressing personal necessity of inner peace and restored consciousness, wounded by his disloyalty to one whom he had fervently regarded as the destined restorer of the holy nation and the holy place, whom he had reverenced as the Son of God, and who, as he could not but feel more and more acutely every hour he recalled all their common life, had deserved that reverence, had never fallen below the ideal standard, had always had something incomprehensible and beyond the grasp of his disciples in his teaching and person!

There is always a gap between the first vision and all subsequent ones: they may be psychologically explained as products of it; the first remains something primitive and original. S. Paul, and all visionaries since (and there have been many), who have seen Jesus, have seen him when the idea of the risen Christ was already established; but the vision, or visions, which established this idea, cannot have been its products.

But is it so certain that this was the first vision of Peter? Was that strange night-scene on the mount of Transfiguration then a sober reality, or has that narrative too a vision of Peter's as its kernel? Was that strange night-apparition on the waters also an unconscious creation of Peter's? (Matt. xiv. 22 ff.; Mark vi. 4 ff.; John vi. 16 ff.) We cannot say more positively than that it might have been so. Peter has the credit of several visions after the Resurrection (Acts x, 10 ff.: xii. 7 ff.), and what have come down to us as events in the life of Christ, which seem to set the physical laws of the universe at defiance, may have had an historical centre of fact quite in accordance with those laws, in the visions of his followers.

It has been said that had we the reports of eye-witnesses of the life of Jesus, they would not differ materially from the reports which we possess; it may be so; but if so, so much the worse for the eye-witnesses' credit. But at least could we cross-question the eye-witnesses, and specially upon this point, of their visions of the risen Master, we should find probably that their accounts were much more ethereal and less loaded with corporeal traits and incidents than the descriptions which we actually possess. We can trace in the case of the last recorded appearance a gradual process of materialization, at least approximately. In Matthew the appearance is apparently a heavenly one, takes place in the open air, and nothing is said descriptive of its coming or going. In Mark the disciples are in a room, the final commission contains some very magical details, and it is expressly said that the Lord was taken up into heaven, though there is no description of the event or process. In the third Gospel the details are enriched, but it is only in the Acts that the Ascension can be said to be properly described, with its accompaniments of cloud and angels. However this may be, it is remarkable that the only notice of a vision of Christ by an eye-witness, S. Paul, gives no details; and as little does S. Paul give details of the other appearances which he records. Could we have cross-questioned Peter or Paul, they would have asserted the reality of their visions, just as stoutly as Joan of Arc when cross-questioned asserted the reality of hers; but they would perhaps have been just as impatient of questions of detail as Joan was, when asked about the size and hair and eyes and so on, of the Archangel Michael. It is one thing to have to do with a vision at first hand; and another, when it has passed awhile from mouth to mouth.

But there always remains a gap, not only between the first vision and any following one, but between the first vision and the antecedents out of which we attempt to account for it. In the particular instance we never come quite to fill up the line of continuity between cause and effect with details; we never grasp the individual in all its individuality, we never reproduce in definition or analysis the full substance and reality of life and existence. But then this is true of every individual reality, near and far; do we therefore in all cases abandon the belief that the unknown is homogeneous with the known, do we open the door to the supernatural?

To explain the vision of Peter as the product of natural causes, we have the negative conditions for a vision arising from the ignorance of the times, from the prevalent ideas current on the subject of supernatural warnings and visitants, and the relations of the spiritual and material worlds to each other, the spiritual world being still conceived as substantially material, and located in a definite place, above the earth; these ideas formed, as it were, the common background of any ordinary Jewish mind of the time. We have, besides, the special circumstances and character of Peter, so far as we can reconstruct them: and it must be admitted that there is a great deal in them to make a vision comprehensible; they go a certain way towards explaining it. And if his vision still remains to us more or less an irrational quantity, shall we ascribe the unamalgamated residuum to our ignorance of all the co-efficients at work in the case, and range this vision with all other visions; or shall we leave it as a problem still, or even grasp at what must now appear an arbitrary and external explanation, and as such indeed, strictly speaking, no explanation at all?

To Peter we may ascribe on S. Paul's authority the first vision of the risen Master. Whether any of the Galilean women had previously visions of Jesus or of angels must remain, on account of the silence of S. Paul, very doubtful. It has been said that the vision of Peter was really the vision of Mary Magdalene, who was the first to behold the risen Christ, but "in consequence of the eternal injustice by which the man appropriates to himself alone the work in which the woman has had just as much part as he, Cephas eclipses Mary, and causes her to be forgotten."* That Mary may have had a vision, not merely as a woman deeply attached to the departed Jesus, but as a woman specially susceptible from a more or less abnormal organism, a woman out of whom, in the scriptural phrase, Jesus had cast seven devils, cannot appear improbable; but there is no sufficient reason for denying the vision to Peter, because Mary may have had one too, any more than for identifying his vision with hers.

We cannot adequately represent to ourselves the state of mind of the disciples in those first days of the over-

---

* Renan, "Les Apôtres," p. 55, cf. p. 11 ff.

throw of their hopes: they could not, we may well believe, settle down to any ordinary occupation; at least till they had in some way or other come to an understanding with the event which had overtaken them. They may well have searched the Scriptures in the hope of finding light on the matter, and they could not search in vain: they may well have fasted and prayed for comfort and guidance in their collapse and bewilderment; and what a light must have come, once the word went forth, "The Lord hath appeared unto Simon!" "The idea of the risen Christ" was therewith not indeed established, but given; and this was enough. It was not long before others also had visions, how frequently we cannot say; the list given by S. Paul must surprise us rather by its brevity than its length, for it is obviously complete according to the best of his knowledge. That several persons should have a vision at once is far from being without parallel. "We know," write the anonymous authors of "The Unseen Universe," "the almost infinite power of the mind not only to delude itself, but to propagate its delusion to the mind of others."* And mere numbers add nothing in such a case to the credibility of a supernatural explanation of the appearance: "if not only a single individual, but several persons, should be 'possessed' by one and the same idea or feeling, the same misinterpretation may be made by all of them; and in such a case the concurrence of their testimony does not add the least strength to it."† There may have been five hundred brethren together on some occasion, but if so they can hardly have been drawn together by any other cause than the report that Jesus had risen; they

---

* Op. cit. p. 42. 1st Edit.   † Carpenter, op. cit. § 187.

were in fact possessed by one and the same idea or feeling, and that they may have seen, some of them or all of them, (for it is not very likely that they were individually cross-questioned) something which they took for an appearance of the risen Lord, is quite possible. A natural object may be mistaken for a supernatural appearance by persons possessed with an idea, and their account of this vision however coherent, is not therefore trustworthy; and the mind unconvinced by the visions of Paul or of Peter cannot be seriously discomposed by the bare assertion that five hundred brethren saw the risen Jesus at once, of whom the greater part were alive when S. Paul wrote—as though he had cross-examined upwards of two hundred and fifty of them!

A great deal is sometimes made of the doubts and unwillingness to believe the fact of the Resurrection which are ascribed to the Apostles in the Gospel record. If they really had any doubts, if this trait in the narrative be not a result of the more or less apologetic consciousness of a later time working on the bare facts for the benefit of those who had not seen and might yet believe; we must not confuse such doubts or misgivings with the critical scepticism of modern science. Joan of Arc also doubted her visions at first, but the mere repetition of the vision was sufficient to persuade her of its truth; and the Apostles were not any more critical than Joan of Arc. Some stress too has been laid on the sober understanding of the Apostles, and on the calm unvarnished character of the narratives; as to the latter, because the narratives are "simple, earnest, cold, almost lifeless," it does not follow that the Apostles were so; as to the former point, there is nothing more interesting than to observe how strong the mind and understanding of visionaries may be, as well in their inferences and deductions from their visions, as also in matters of daily life; it was so, again, with Joan, it was so with Savonarola; and indeed a certain strength of mind is necessary perhaps before a man can have a vision at all, most of all where the vision is more or less the effect of an idea.

There is a further point upon which Apologists insist, viz. that three days were too short a time for all the psychological process necessary to produce a vision, for the thought and reflection on the events, on the previous life with Jesus, on his Messianic claims, on the Old Testament prophecies. In his first "Leben Jesu" Strauss represented the origin of the belief in the Resurrection as a process of reflection on what must have happened, Jesus being the Messias, and on the right interpretation of Scripture, a specimen of which is preserved to us in the second chapter of the Acts. But such a conscious process of reflection had probably in the case of the first believers little or nothing to do with the production of their visions; though, once the visions had taken place, such a process must have had full play, and being conducted to prove the truth of the Resurrection of the Messias, a foregone conclusion, the proof was naturally conclusive; nor was there any principle of interpretation among the Jews of the day which could invalidate the Apostolic exegesis. It must however be noticed that it cannot really be admitted as at all an established fact that the first appearance of the risen Christ took place on the third day, though it may be agreed that it did not take place before. The *doctrine* is that Christ rose again the third day; but even on this point there is not a fixed manner of expression in our documental sources.* Three

* τῇ τρίτῃ ἡμέρᾳ, 1 Cor. xv. 4; as also Matt. and Luke. μετὰ τρεῖς

days was a proverbial Jewish expression for a short period; but there were also special allusions in the Old Testament which might have suggested this number (Hosea vi. 2), and the typical case of the prophet Jonah (Matt. xii. 39 ff.) by a misinterpretation perhaps of words of Jesus' own, may have been made to suit it. It was also a belief of the Jews that the departed soul remained in the neighbourhood of the dead body for three days, and then sought the underworld.* There seems an uncertainty in the tradition as to the exact time at which Jesus rose; the earlier form represents the Resurrection as taking place, as we should say, on Saturday evening, the later on Sunday morning; the preference for the latter being due perhaps to its making the great event coincide with the dawn of the natural day and of the Christian Sunday.† Thus the belief was that Jesus rose on the third day, and the natural supposition was that he appeared on the same day on which he rose; but S. Paul does not say so expressly, nor does he give any distinct temporal any more than local details of the appearances which he enumerates. Keim notices that the journey to Galilee takes just three days, and that only in Galilee could so many as five hundred disciples have come together; but just as we cannot be quite sure whether the appearances took place in Jerusalem or in Galilee, or some perhaps in the one, some in the other, so we cannot be quite sure whether or not the first vision took place on the third day. It may have done so; and if it did, this was a reason more for the belief that Jesus had

---

ἡμέρας, Mark viii. 31, ix. 31, x. 34. Cf. Rev. xi. 11, μετὰ τὰς τρεῖς ἡμέρας καὶ ἥμισυ.

* Keim, iii. p. 549. † So Keim.

risen on the third day. This is as much as we can say definitely.

We return here naturally upon the narrative that the grave was found empty on the third day. But we have already found so many difficulties about the empty grave of Jesus that even the fact has become suspect. The doubt can only be increased by the reflection that the visions of the Apostles took place perhaps in Galilee. It is sometimes said that if the grave had not been found empty the Jews would have refuted the Apostles' announcement of the Resurrection of their Master, by producing the dead body. But before this announcement can have come to the ears of the Jewish authorities the body was already unrecognizable; and it is also very doubtful whether the production of the body would have been a refutation of the assertion of the Apostles. It would have been no difficulty, as we have seen, to the doctrine of Paul; and if the primitive Apostles had less clear theories of the nature of Christ's Person, yet the visions would have had absolute validity for them, and would have helped them to form the conception of the spiritual body in distinction from the earthy. But this idea of the production of the dead body to refute the Apostles shows a want of historical appreciation of the state of thought at the time. So current was the notion of Resurrection, in some form or other, that Herod is represented as mistaking Jesus for the risen John Baptist (Matt. xiv. 2). Did Antipas or his servants settle the question of John's resurrection by examining his grave? And what would it have profited, when the Jews believed that after three days a corpse was unrecognizable?* The Christian imagination must take the

* Keim, iii. p. 549.

credit of many details, consciously or unconsciously incorporated with the primitive tradition, as well from the inevitable tendency to idealize (according to its own canons of idealization) the original Figure of its Head, as in order to refute popular objections, sure to be of the crudest and most materialistic type. Is it inconceivable that this imaginative activity should have produced the whole story of the empty grave? In the accounts of the burial we may observe a growing tendency to exaggerate details which might be supposed to contribute to the honour of Jesus; yet in presence of Paul's express assertion that Jesus was buried, (though he only makes it on the authority of hearsay,) and in view of the actual importance of burial in the eyes of Jews, it may be admitted as most probable that Jesus was laid in a grave by the hands of some friends. And so it must remain an open question whether or not the grave was afterwards found empty; if it was, and the body removed by the hands of foes or friends, unknown to the other disciples of Jesus, then the discovery of the empty grave was one more cause for the speedy growth of the belief that the Lord had risen, though not an indispensable cause for the growth of that belief. It must always remain an open question whether the discovery of the empty sepulchre helped to produce the idea of the risen Christ, or the idea of the risen Christ produced the story of the empty sepulchre.

What emerges from the discussion as a common admission is that there were visions among the friends of Jesus shortly after his death, which they explained from the idea of Resurrection. That they should do so was almost inevitable, for they were imbued with the current notions of their age and nation; and given their previous belief in Jesus as the Messias, and the fact of his death, his reappearance could only be his Resurrection. Jesus, himself, who, while perpetually insisting on the moral and spiritual truths which held the first place in his consciousness, was still not in all respects so far above his time and circumstances but that he must have used the common language, and shared some common ignorance or illusions with the people about him, may have used language during his life, which when recalled and interpreted in the light of his Resurrection looked like a prophecy of the event, and thus in the minds of the Apostles confirmed at once the fact of the Resurrection, and the Messiasship of their Master. But however this may be, no one will be found to assert that the Resurrection of Jesus was the introduction of this idea into human consciousness; on the contrary the idea of a Resurrection, not indeed of the Messias himself, but of the Jews to take part in his kingdom, and even of a Second Resurrection, of the just and unjust to judgment, was a commonplace in Jewish thought at the time.* The belief of the Apostles in the Resurrection was the result of the process which we have already twice described as the process in every case where we become convinced of a new fact or doctrine, of the truth of a new proposition; it was the expression of the adjustment effected in their consciousness, between a mass of ideas already therein more or less systematized, and a new fact or group of facts, the appearances, the visions of their Master. That he whom they had firmly believed to be the expected Deliverer should die, and die on the cross, that was startling, and seemed to cut at the roots of all

* Bertholdt: "Christologia Judæorum Jesu Apostolorumque tempore," §§ 35-41.

their most cherished preconvictions; and a struggle must have ensued between this fact and those preconvictions, and the Disciples must either have modified the latter, or resigned their belief and love for their Master, which yet they could not do, all the less, the more the full influence of his teaching and personality reasserted itself. But the further fact of his Resurrection restored harmony to their distracted minds and feelings; he was crucified, and yet the Messias. And that they should interpret the appearances which presented themselves, not as products of their own mental and moral excitement, working within the doctrinal lines furnished by the theology and psychology of their day, but as objective supernatural Christophanies; this was predetermined by these very doctrinal lines. The first believers may be said to have been converted by the Resurrection of Jesus, but it was a slight conversion compared even with the change wrought in S. Paul; and so was not immediately fruitful for the world; and their highest service to humanity perhaps has been that they formed an indispensable condition for the conversion of the Apostle of the Gentiles. They created, or carried on from Jesus himself, the idea of a suffering and crucified Messias, which became to Paul the new moral revelation of God's plan of salvation: but they never grasped the significance of this fact themselves; they never reformed, so completely as Paul did, the Jewish expectations and preconceptions of the work and office of the Messias, which they shared with him, and with the majority of their nation. They had believed Jesus to be the Messias, and had therefore attached to his Person those floating popular expectations; his death shook for the moment their confidence that he it was that should restore the kingdom to Israel in their day, but did not alter their Messianic ideas themselves: with the appearances, which they interpreted by the idea of Resurrection familiar to them, their relation to their Messias was restored, their hopes revived, and they could now wait in hope and joy for his return in power and glory to establish the Messianic kingdom, for which it was now their function to prepare the way by preaching repentance to the people, among whom they expected shortly to sit, each on a throne, in judgment. These crude and partial conceptions of the future may well have been intensified and further defined by opposition to the new convert, who, without ever having known Jesus personally, claimed to be an Apostle, not merely a subordinate fellow-worker with the Twelve; and it needed not merely the actual success of the preaching of Paul (which was to a Jew the sign of the divine approval,) but the actual destruction of Jerusalem (A.D. 70), to make the Jewish preconceptions of the early Christians give way to accomplished facts. Nay, we cannot say that they ever properly speaking gave way, in the sense that the primitive Jewish Christians altered their doctrine to suit events; the centre of Christianity was shifted from Jerusalem to Antioch, to Rome, to Alexandria, and Christianity itself underwent corresponding modifications; and Jerusalem never regained importance, as a centre of orthodox Christianity, until the pious attention of the western Church made it the bourn for pilgrims.*

But neither the change accomplished in S. Paul nor the change accomplished in the primitive Apostles carried them out of their most fundamental methods of conceiving God, and the Soul, and the World. In both

---

* "Ce lieu a toujours été anticrétien."—Renan, "Vie de Jesu," 224.

cases no doubt a profound moral change in consciousness took place; but the change was conditioned by the physical and psychological, yes and the metaphysical notions of the subjects of the change. They interpreted the facts of their experience by the doctrines already in their mind; are we to do the same?

But what are the doctrines in our mind? Did we not start in doubt as it were between two sets of conflicting doctrine, or opinion, the one or the other of which we were to choose according as the Resurrection turned out to be a fact or not a fact? And now what do we find but that in order to be assured that the Resurrection is a fact we must have, it seems, a body of doctrines already held for true in our minds?

The state of the case seems to be this: there are two sets of doctrine, two views "of the whole universe, of all being and of all life, of man and of the world and of God;" either of these views fits in with the facts, but not both of them; they are neither of them, at least on the first glance, inconsistent with the facts, but they are inconsistent with each other, and cannot therefore both be true. The admitted fact is that the Apostles believed Jesus to have risen from the dead. The explanation of this fact according to the one view comes out as the statement that he did miraculously rise; on the other view, that the Apostles, from their standpoint must inevitably have believed him to be risen. Is our standpoint the same as theirs?

This very claim to explain the appearances of the risen Christ out of their natural antecedents is a fact which meets *us*, which *we* have to digest as best we may. Just as the assertion that the faith of the early believers in the Resurrection was due to the fact of the Resurrection, or to the reality, the transcendental reality, of the appearances of the risen Jesus, is an assertion coherent with one view of the universe, so the assertion that this belief was due to natural antecedents, without the immediate intervention of any supernatural causality, is coherent with another view of the universe: and thus it appears that the ultimate fact in question, viz., the Resurrection, remains still in question, until we have settled which view of the universe we are to adopt. That is to say, in order to decide the nature of the cardinal fact or event of Christianity, we must already have a view of the universe: do the doctrines of Christianity not constitute such a view? And if they do, what becomes of the assertion that the doctrines of Christianity flow from alleged facts? What then does the allegation of the facts flow from?

In truth the two sets of doctrines lie before us; if the one set is true, Jesus rose from the dead; if it is not true, or if the other set is true, he did not rise from the dead; but how are we to decide between the two conflicting and fundamental views? What has the one or the other to say in its own favour?

The one may claim to be more or less nearly the view held by the Apostles themselves, and by the majority of Christians since, at least when pressed to state their theoretical views of God, the Soul, and the World. The other may claim to be a view that is habitually acted upon in daily life, that is presupposed in all science, and in all popular knowledge, which differs from science not so much in kind as in degree. It may also claim to have constantly won ground from its rival. Above all, it may claim to be consistent with itself in practice; whereas the advocates of the other view are guilty of perpetual inconsistencies, for they introduce a principle of disunion and confusion into the universe, fatal to the first principle of continuity, a first principle to which they nevertheless pay daily practical homage, in every step of life when they trust the order of nature and their own intelligence either in theory or practice: so that they are constantly acting and reasoning upon principles at fundamental discord with their own view of the universe, a view which is indeed destructive of thought and action, for if carried out, it amounts to absolute scepticism or absolute quietism. The view, which we may call that of critical philosophy, further rests itself on the appeal to verification; whereas the other is not open to verification at all, and must therefore appeal to authority, as it does not even make a show of a living revelation in the present.* This appeal to authority involves it in fresh contradictions, since this authority can after all itself only be justified by an appeal to reason, by subjecting itself to criticism; so that nothing but "permanent mental confusion" could be the result of this view of the universe, if it were clearly comprehended and acted upon by its advocates.

Whence comes it then that the rival theory is not accepted? What are the intellectual causes which keep in existence a theory apparently so obsolete in itself, and so destructive of all logical consistency in thought?

* This is true at least of Anglican and Protestant Apologetics. The superior Logic of the Roman Church will be indicated in the sequel.

CHAPTER III.

FACT AND ILLUSION: FIRST PRINCIPLES AND FAITH.

CRITICISM may go a long way in "explaining" the belief of the Apostles in the Resurrection, in explaining their visions as not different in origin or psychological form from any visions of which a healthy human organism can be the subject; and yet it seems still as far as ever from gaining assent to its analysis, as far as ever from satisfying the intelligence of the average Christian that its conclusions are really true or even probable; though his instinct or imagination is quick to grasp the supposed bearings of criticism on life and morality, which, it may be admitted, are of the gravest and most alarming character.

And yet, for good or for ill, Criticism must have the best of the argument, from the nature of the case; it must win a game, where, with the consent of its adversary, or whether he consent or not, it has the making of the rules; and where the game consists in the adversary assuming the defensive, and only surrendering piece after piece as slowly as possible, till Criticism is left complete master of the intellectual field. The same story repeats itself in every fresh case of surrender; Criticism gives check; the Apologist invokes a *Deus ex machina*; Criticism says, Such intervention puts an end to the game, for it is against the rules which constitute the game, and to these you have given at least implicit assent, by entering the lists at all; the Apologist gives up his "mechanical theory" with the best grace he can, or makes room for a brother Apologist, a degree or two more initiated in the skill of the game, who discards the "mechanical theory" with as much impatience or pity as the hottest critic, and makes his move, sublimely unconscious that the same fate awaits himself which has befallen his predecessor: he too will receive his check; he too will appeal, if not to the Church's infallibility, if not to the mechanical theory of inspiration, still to his own *Deus ex machina*, perhaps "Faith." Criticism will repeat, "Against the rules of the game; why did you come here to play?" and his place will be taken by another, who finds one piece less on the board.

Revelation and its correlative Faith are indeed, in one form or other, always the powers outside the game to which the appeal is made when a piece becomes forfeit; and one might be tempted, in forgetfulness of the ingenuity of the human mind, to think that this appeal has now been made for the last time. It has come to this; the historical event, *imprimis*, the Resurrection of Jesus on the third day from the dead, is the Revelation—all else is to be deduced from this, by the ordinary processes of criticism: leave us one supernatural event, and that is our basis from which we can reconstruct the whole revelation; that one fact contains in itself implicitly the whole. But how are we to convince ourselves of the truth of this one fact? The answer often is, and wisely is, by Faith. Unfortunately, however, we find ourselves here in a glaring contradiction: Criticism says, The historical event can only be vouched for by my canons; an event cannot be at once historical and super-

8 *

natural, for history is only possible on the presupposition of the absolute continuity and homogeneity of experience; and that presupposition is uprooted and annihilated by the presupposition of Revelation. Thus what you here call Faith is a presupposition which renders my whole existence null; and you should not have sat down to play with me at all. On the other hand, if you admit that the historical supernatural event is to be attested by my own canons, the contradiction is only the more apparent: nothing enters the realm of history, as constituted by me, save through the gates of nature : you are moving a piece otherwise than the laws of the game admit, you cannot save the piece; surrender it, or make way for another player.*

To make use of our metaphor a little further: it is the history of the game itself which is peculiarly instructive.

* For a remarkable confirmation of the view taken in this Essay of the relations between facts and doctrine, as well as for additional support of the explanation offered of the Apostolic visions, I should like to refer my readers to an article by Dr. Carpenter in the "Contemporary Review," January, 1876, entitled, "The fallacies of testimony in relation to the Supernatural." Dr. Carpenter's polemic against the Supernatural is indeed of a character all but purely empirical. He admits the possibility of miracles; he only questions the credibility of the historical evidence. This is a very reasonable ground to take in a popular polemic : most persons perhaps are Theists of one sort or another, all with a growing respect for science : and this is the position of "the Scientific Theist," as Dr. Carpenter calls him (op. cit. p. 281). Many will resign Miracles and Revelation, but still cling to dogmatic Theism, for a long time. But any one who considers more deeply the question of the possibility of history—in every sense of the word—will probably come to the conclusion that it is only possible upon the basis of that principle of continuity, which is irreconcilable with miracles ; that if miracles are possible, history is impossible; and that *historical* evidence for miracles is nothing short of a contradiction in terms.

We see the Apologist when compelled by the presupposition of criticism to resign one position after another, still go on to defend the positions left him, first with the aid of criticism, so far as it appears to lend him a shield or even a spear; and then by an appeal to the presupposition of faith, when the ground is cut from under his feet, in virtue of the very principles which he professes to recognize. The real controversy does not lie, therefore, anywhere else than between the presuppositions; the utterly false position of the modern Apologist consists in this, that he is not in earnest with either presupposition, but tries to combine them, though they are no more to be combined than oil and vinegar. The practical result is that he goes a mile with his man, but will not go twain; he is always harking back to a road, which if it start from the same centre, goes out into space in a diametrically opposite direction. He is not thoroughgoing with his criticism, and he is not thoroughgoing with his faith. To be the latter is indeed a sheer impossibility, for as the presuppositions of criticism, or rationalized experience, are exactly the same as the presuppositions of ordinary everyday experience and human life, the Apologist can scarcely be anything in his theories but a half and half philosopher, where the two halves are heterogeneous: and must help himself out of the dilemma, as best he can, by the assumption of two truths, the one philosophic, the other theological; or of a Yes from the practical reason where the theoretical reason has said No; or of light in Faith where man's science threatens to extinguish God's revelation; or by the assumption of some other dualistic theory which virtually maintains that Truth is to be found by combining the conclusions of Dogmatism and Scepticism.

In any case his theory and his practice must stand in contradiction to each other; for we only live in security so long and in so far as we behave as rational beings; and our freest thoughts, our most unconscious acts pay homage to the reason in things, and in ourselves; the laws given, which shall not be broken.

It is for these reasons:—because the presupposition of Supernaturalism cuts at the root of all experience, whether in *esse* or in *posse*, whether codified in science or unconsciously gathered and applied in life; and because the history of the struggle between criticism and its adversary shows the self-condemnation of the latter;—that we must throw in our lot with the younger child of Time, and believe that he is destined to supplant the elder. Supernaturalism is perpetually stultifying itself by selling its birthright, and making all sorts of suicidal concessions to its younger brother. We can reconstruct, after a fashion, its title deeds, from the history of these concessions. It still claims the Father's blessing; we can show what this claim logically presupposes, and how this presupposition has long ago been voluntarily abandoned.

What we are now asked to spare is a supernatural historical phenomenon, as source of Christian doctrine. But such an event is at variance with ordinary historical criticism; as this criticism, therefore, cannot be applied to the record or evidence for the event without producing in our minds the negation of the event, to preserve the phenomenon we must exempt the record from strict criticism, we must not treat the Bible as we treat other books;* we must

* Cp. the words addressed to the University of Oxford by a preacher, now Professor of the Exegesis of Holy Scripture: "Woe to you, if they (philology, history, geography) persuade you to read the Book of Life as a Pagan might read it, as you your-

hold fast the doctrine of Inspiration in some form or other, which shall make a qualitative difference between the Bible and all other books, or collection of books. But it is quite obvious that even the inspired book, or literature rather, is capable of widely different interpretations, and the Faith which demands an inspired record of supernatural events, will require further an infallible authority for the correct interpretation of the record; all the more so, as the record is not merely a record, but also a treasury of doctrine. So we come back from the necessity of a past supernatural event to the necessity of a present supernatural Church, at least for all who do not claim for themselves an immediate divine revelation; for all, that is, who acknowledge that the Truth comes to them mediately. But this logical process of construction, which might very well lead an earnest dialectical mind, once convinced of the necessity of a special revelation, to pass over to the Church of Rome, is just the reverse of the process which has accomplished itself in the progressive mind of Europe since the Reformation. Protestantism in discarding the supernatural claims and authority of the Church, was far from applying its own principle universally; partly no doubt because the Reformation was in its beginning more a moral than an intellectual protest and uprising, partly because the full bearings even of intellectual principles are never seen at first; and as has been well said, though in quite a different connection, to judge of the doctrine we must look not to the Master but to the scholars. The first effect of the Reformation was indeed to force out a more definite position and authority for the Scriptures, and the

selves might read Herodotus or Plato."—Liddon: "University Sermons X." (5th Ed. p. 278.)

so-called "mechanical doctrine of Inspiration," of which our liberal Apologists now-a-days make such short work, was a product as natural and necessary in its day, and with as definite a purpose to serve as their own vaguer appeals to Faith or Instinct.* It may have served its

* In his "Gospel of the Resurrection," Dr. Westcott's Court of Appeal seems to be Instinct; *e.g.* p. 12. "The authority of testimony is supplemented by that of the *instinct* within us which recognizes the harmony of a Revelation claiming to be Divine with the essential wants of man." The claim to be divine is made by all Religions, and so far therefore as this is concerned, Instinct says as much for one as for any other; and the inference is: The more a religion corresponds to the essential wants of man, the more likely it is to be a natural product, even if an unconscious, and in so far instinctive, product of human wishes and thoughts concurring with external conditions. It is also, however, rapidly becoming, if not already become, an essential want of man, to examine his instincts, all of them, whether original or acquired, whether spontaneous, or mixed with reflection, with a view of controlling, and if need be, altering them by the light of his maturest reason and experience.

P. 40. "It is, indeed, a mystery wholly beyond our comprehension how an infinite Being can reveal or in any way manifest Himself to finite creatures. But in obedience to an instinct which we cannot question we have taken it for granted that he does so." Why cannot we question it? Of course we can, we ought to question it; and both Reason and History have a word to say on the subject of this so-called instinct, which is no instinct at all, but only the logical necessity to assume a premise for a foregone conclusion.

P. 146. "There is indeed an imperious instinct which affirms that *we* shall survive death," etc.

How a theological doctrine may come in course of time to look like spontaneous faith! Most thoughtful people understand by instinct something spontaneous, active, and above all unconscious, something which produces results often in a high degree artful (so to speak) without design. But we need not press a correct terminology. To refer a doctrine, a theory, a hope to instinct (or was it Christianity which brought Immortality to light?) as the final ground of belief, shows strange oversight in a work which

purpose, at least of stopping a gap against Rome, but as it is essentially arbitrary, it must submit in turn to the same law of disintegration which proves too much for the authority of the Church. The supernatural authority of the Bible is given up in turn, and we are invited to apply to it the ordinary processes of Criticism, Faith (so-called) having taken refuge in the assumption that though the record may be natural the event will remain supernatural. Vain assumption! The process of disintegration must proceed, and the event must be recognized as natural, as well as the record.

But what is the event to be recognized as natural? Not surely the fact that Jesus Christ rose from the dead? It is indeed conceivable that persons very imperfectly acquainted with the comparative history of religions, with the state of belief and opinions in the first century of our era, and with the psychological conditions of belief in general, should suppose that Jesus really rose from the

sets "relation to reason and history" on its title page. What does History show, if not that the education of man consists to no small extent in bringing his "imperious" instinct under the yoke of Reason?

However it would seem that Dr. Westcott on occasion knows that our instincts, real or misnamed, are not in themselves final authorities, for he says of another "instinct" that the "Scripture first teaches us to believe that the instinct is true" (p. 172).

One does not at first know what teaches us to accept Scripture as bail for our instinct; perhaps another instinct, ... and so on *ad infinitum.*

After all this it is strange to hear of belief in Christ that it has not only "interpreted" but also "conquered this and that instinctive feeling" (p. 245). What then renders any instinct imperious or unquestionable? Not its being instinct at any rate.

It is unfortunate that Dr. Westcott should adopt as a speculative authority a power which is supposed specially to be rooted in the natural, but unconscious, action of mind and nerves; and is not safely to be appealed to on theoretical questions.

grave on the third day ; and in the acknowledged obscurity of the relations between spirit and matter, both of which enter into all natural processes, it might be hypothetically maintained that this Resurrection, as a strictly natural event, and in no sense miraculous, did take place. This sort of appeal *ad ignorantiam* could not in any case justify more than a suspension of judgment, or a negative hypothesis; as the event seems probable on historical grounds, it may be that there are powers in nature, or rather moments where spirit has such all but omnipotence over matter, that functions of life which had been interrupted and replaced by the process of dissolution, might be resumed, and dissolution reversed. But such an hypothesis is too obviously in the air, and, as it is utterly devoid of all support in analogy, could not maintain itself against the strong negative improbability. In the light of experience it must remain more probable that the Apostles were in error than that such an event took place ; add the considerations drawn from what we know of them, their state of mind, hopes, opinions; and the strong negative improbability of the one event, hitherto deemed supernatural, but in the present case *ex hypothesi* natural, becomes a positive argument in favour of the rival fact, or supposed fact, viz. that the belief of the Apostles in the Resurrection was a purely natural product, but not due to the objective reality of the alleged fact.

Such is the conclusion of philosophical criticism, but it is not generally acceptable : much of what is best and most humane in us, our so-called moral instincts, seem to rise against such a conclusion. They furnish us with an argument of a teleological character against the theory that a belief in the Resurrection was due to natural antecedents, one of which was not the fact in question: in other words, that it was an erroneous inference, however unconscious, on the part of the first believers, which has propagated itself in the world, ever since. The influence of the belief upon the Apostles in the first instance, and through them upon the world, or that part of it which has come under the influence of Christianity, is pointed out; and we are asked whether such results, and such results for good, can be due to an illusion?

Now it must be remarked here, in the first place, that given a belief of the same intensity, its results remain exactly the same, whether it is an illusion or an accurate reproduction of facts. Leaving out of account beliefs which lead to acts hostile or destructive to human society; of those which have been productive of the greatest benefits to nations or individuals, how many have been true, in a scientific sense? How many have not been better than the truth? What we wish for, that we believe to be good; and what is good, must be true; this is the epitome of Faith's genesis.* Our ideals are always untrue, measured by experience; they are anticipations of experience, and they remain, many of them, anticipations which experience teaches us were not merely ideals but illusions. But an illusion, if it is strong, can produce good fruit for the whole world, if only the illusion be the expression of the best wish in the world at the time. And the best wish which the Apostles could have was that their Master should be with them to the end of the world. What if the wish, the necessity,

---

* Constat itaque . . . . nihil nos conari, velle, appetere neque cupere, quia id bonum esse judicamus; sed contra nos propterea aliquid bonum esse judicare, quia id conamur, volumus, appetimus atque cupimus.—Spinoza, " Eth. III., ix. Schol."

working in conjunction with the other motives analyzed previously, should have produced the belief? or how could the belief realize itself save in the forms supplied to it by the knowledge and opinions of the time and of the men? The truth is that the Master was with them, if not in the body, yet in power and spiritual presence, far more after death than before; the illusion was only the form in which this real presence expressed itself in the first instance.

We cannot easily bear to acknowledge to ourselves that the Apostles were subject to an illusion in respect to the Reappearance of their departed Master and the inference based thereupon; and yet we make little difficulty perhaps out of another illusion to which they were as certainly subject, and which stood in near relation to the former, although it lies now so far from us, the belief in his Second Advent. There is perhaps no point at which the difference between the primitive Church and the mass of modern Christians makes itself more conspicuously manifest than this. Those who wish to identify their form of Christianity with that of the first believers, by raising the fact of the Resurrection into supreme prominence, should remember that the certainty of the Parusia, or Second Coming of Christ, and that in their own day, was an element in the primitive Creed of Christians no less essential. If the Resurrection had value for them, it was primarily an evidential value which it had; it restored their confidence that Jesus was the Messias, and this confidence was the whole faith of primitive Christianity, and the novelty of it was not contained in the predicate but in the subject of the sentence.* The

---

* Reuss, op. cit. § 29.

doctrine that Jesus was the Messias was the only dogma, so to speak, by which primitive Christianity separated itself from Judaism, or at least from the beliefs and hopes of the bulk of the Jewish people. The Apostles carried over into Christianity all the opinions, beliefs, and expectations connected with the Messias which they had been familiar with as Jews; and it was, as we have seen above, in the first instance the genius of Paul, working upon the given fact of the death of the Messias, and secondly the Christian consciousness of a later time, which has found its sublime representative in the author of the fourth Gospel, working upon the given fact that the apostolic age had passed away, and still the Millennium was not come, which profoundly modified the Christian conception of the Messias, his work, and his kingdom.

The Bible is so habitually read in the light of preconceptions of a dogmatic character, and such preconceptions have so disturbing an effect upon the historical sense, that there are still persons to be found who deny that the Apostles and early Christians definitely anticipated the end of the world and the second coming of Christ in their own day, or allowed such an expectation to affect their conduct in any way or degree other than the thought of his Advent, and the uncertainty of the day and hour of his appearance, should affect devout believers in the present day. This one-sided and subjective and at the same time dogmatical assertion, which we may expect from persons of strong ecclesiastical bias who have Church history at their backs, may be corrected in a way by the more naïve interpretation, no less subjective and one-sided, of those of a more "evangelical" bias, who look more or less confidently for the reappearance of Jesus Christ in the clouds at no distant day. The latter undoubtedly represent the early Christians more accurately in this respect; for the primitive Church looked for the Return of its Master, not merely at some wholly indefinite time in the future, but before long, in a short time, quickly, soon. Now-a-days those who hold to this belief, and its kindred notion of a Millennium, or Reign of Christ on earth for a thousand years, ground their faith chiefly on the book of Revelation. It is undoubtedly most clearly expressed in this book, the earliest work in the New Testament which can be connected with the primitive Christianity of Jerusalem; but the same ideas and expectations underlie all the writings of the New Testament, the Johannine works perhaps alone excepted, and form unmistakably a presupposition for the right understanding of Pauline Christianity, however much Paul's Gospel may be in secret already developed and raised above the level and limits of such conceptions. Paul was a Pharisee, and transferred to Jesus the pharisaic ideas connected with the Messias, the two Resurrections, the thousand years' reign, the last trumpet, the judgment, the renewal of all things. But certainly with Paul these ideas held a different rank to that assigned to them by the primitive believers; for Paul, as already shown, was the first to grasp the significance of the Crucifixion of the Messias; and the practical consequences of the doctrine which he deduced from the given fact were very different to the practice of the Church in Jerusalem. But reflection on the consequences of the death of the Messias was not of itself sufficient to transform the eschatology of the primitive Church; it required the might of external facts, on the one hand the negative fact of the delay and non-fulfilment of the expectation of a speedy Restitution of all things, of the Restitution of the Kingdom to Israel;

on the other hand the positive fact of the destruction of Jerusalem, to discredit the primitive conception on this head. Paul did not live to witness the confirmation of his thought and work contained in the fact of the destruction of Jerusalem, though it can hardly be doubtful that he would have grasped the significance of this event, and its bearing upon traditional doctrine, as he had grasped the significance of the Death of Christ. But it could hardly have been given to him to modify the primitive conception of the kingdom of the Messias more profoundly than the author of the Epistle and Gospel which bear the name of John has modified that conception. However that may be, his eschatology is the one point where we can still see in Paul a development, more or less pronounced, after his appearance as a Christian Apostle. In his earlier Epistles he writes in the unquestioning assurance that he himself will live to see the Return of his Master in glory: in his Roman prison, with the memory of his activity and sufferings for the Gospel behind him, with the shadow of death already perhaps upon him, he is divided between the wish to depart and the wish to remain, for to depart is to be with Christ immediately. But what was thus to Paul at last become for his own person an external and accidental conception, which did not further or impede his union with Christ in life and death, had remained for the primitive Jewish Christians, as may still be seen in the New Testament itself, one of the main elements of their faith and source of their hope and strength. Either Jesus himself had given some countenance to these hopes, or his immediate disciples had, perhaps quite unconsciously, given words of his a twist into accordance with their own more materialistic expectations, and missed the deeper spiritual truth which he may have meant to convey to those who had ears to hear. However this may be, we have before us the spectacle of men finding divine sustenance and support, amid danger and persecution from their own countrymen, and with the prospect of their country's complete overthrow already before their eyes, in an idea and order of ideas which we must now pronounce illusions: the Lord did not come, the generation passed away, and all things were not fulfilled as they had expected.

But it may be said; There is a great difference in illusions. It is one thing to believe that a man has risen from the grave and ascended into heaven; it is another thing to believe that he will come again and that shortly. The one is an assertion of accomplished facts, based on the testimony of the senses; the other is an assertion of facts still to be accomplished, based on inference from popular beliefs and from words of the Master himself. The one is history, the other is prophecy; and while an error or illusion in the latter may be put down to human fallibility or misconception, such an error in the former, if it were possible, would look like a deception practised on man by God himself; we cannot credit it.

There is a difference in illusions; but what is the difference worth? The senses can deceive us no less than the judgment; or rather perhaps more accurately said, it is in every case the judgment, be it a conscious or an unconscious judgment, which deceives itself, as to the causes and relations of external things. Granted that the Apostles saw their Master in a glorified form after he had been crucified, dead and already some days, that of him which was mortal, buried: the appearance was real enough, the affection of their organs of sense was real;

it was the judgment which they, were it instinctively or after discussion among themselves, and with comparison of other experiences, based upon the appearance which was erroneous. If any one now-a-days has a vision of a departed friend, probably he puts it down to physiological and psychological causes, and might very well welcome it as a spontaneous testimony of his own nature to the worth of his friend, and to his own love and loyalty to the departed one. The Apostles interpreted their visions from the standpoint of their own unreflecting realism, or of a scepticism as natural and unreflective. There may very well have been doubts at first, but they were not the doubts of a modern man of science; they were only such as a repetition of the vision, as a confirmation from others, as a sympathetic enthusiasm, would convert into assurance. It has been said (as above noticed) that had we really the testimony of eye-witnesses to the life of Jesus, the testimony would not be very different to that which we actually possess: the statement is fairly open to question, and it is nowhere more questionable than in so far as it might be applied to the supposed *post mortem* life of Jesus on earth. The visionary character of the appearances of the Lord is indicated abundantly even in the records as we have them; had we the testimony of eye-witnesses in all cases, as we have in the case of Paul, we can hardly doubt that the records would be as indefinite and telltale as Paul's authentic accounts of his own visions; and could we cross-examine the witnesses, as Joan of Arc was cross-examined—or rather not so, not from theological motives of suspicion and anxiety to show a case of witchcraft or black arts, but from the pure curiosity, to put it on its lowest ground, of human science—should we not find them as unwilling and unable to describe the material details of the visions as she was? Perhaps not quite so unable: for Joan of Arc's imagination was but stored with the memory of pictures of the Angels and Madonna, such as she had seen in churches, and this was the stuff from which her visions were composed: the Apostles and Mary of Magdala had the memory of a living person, his familiar gestures and voice, to form a nucleus for the unconscious construction of a vision, indistinguishable to them from an objective appearance; and for all that, the appearances were visionary and ghostly in their comings and goings, and best recognized in the breaking of bread, or the well-known voice.

We have already cleared our minds of the fallacy that the fact is something hard and fast outside and independent of the judgment; and the relation between our sense and our judgment is very like that between the fact and the doctrine which is supposed to flow from it: the doctrine has been at the making of the fact, and every perception is already a judgment. Joan of Arc when asked how she recognized the Archangel Michael as such, before he made himself known to her, answers: "because I saw him with my bodily eyes." The fishermen of Galilee were hardly more heroic or less naïve than the peasant girl of Domremy; and her visions were of more service to her "Fair France," than the visions of the Apostles to the Chosen land and city. The liberation of Palestine was not indeed then the event predestined and necessary for the progress of the world, or the coming of the Kingdom; but it may be ascribed to the illusions of the early Christians upon this point that they took no active part in the patriotic struggle of their kinsfolk against the Romans. They looked for a supernatural deliverance, they watched the heavens for the sign of the

Son of Man coming in his glory, and all the holy Angels with him: and their illusion respecting the future was part and parcel of their illusion about the past, and had ultimately one root with it in their identification of their Master with the Messias, and their consequent transference to him of all the attributes and functions which their countrymen ascribed to the expected Saviour; with a difference, that for the Christians the glorious coming of the Christ was a second coming, and so naturally looked for more definitely and confidently in the immediate future, than could be the single coming of the Messias Ben-David awaited by the Jews.

As there are two broad paths of science, the inductive and deductive, so there are two fundamental tendencies in art, of which the end of the one is the idealization of the real world, the end of the other, the realization, in an artistic sense, of the ideal world: and just as the methods of science are but the conscious and rationalized counterparts of the forms of inference which men employ daily and hourly on objects of all sorts; so are the results of art but due to the processes of imagination to be observed in less concentrated and specific forms in the general mind of man, of a people, of an age, of a community. Just as the common sense, which is the common science, can set in circulation its proverbs and wise sayings, and is always the conservator of a certain amount of knowledge and judgment and rationalized experience, so the common imagination provides ideals for the life and enthusiasm of societies, whether the ideals be in the past or in the future. In either case the forms of the ideal are borrowed from the actual world; but it results from the nature of these relations that an idealized history or person seems to have a nearer relation to concrete reality than a future state of better things, brought near to us by an imagination which can only work in the material supplied by the present and the past. And so it is easy to persuade ourselves that prophecy is illusive even while history is true, and we fail perhaps to note it when both are really presented to us by the same spirit working with the same tools and the same stuff. We take the Apostolical picture and representation of the Christ, conveyed though it be in the terms of Jewish thought and belief, and we reject the Apostolical picture of the glory of the Christ, which is conveyed to us in the same terms, and belongs to the same general standpoint; and we modify the picture of the Last Things down to the forms and colours permitted by our later common sense, enriched, or at least augmented, by the experience of centuries, and the collapse of many ideals.

So be it: Wisdom is justified of all her works: the idealized past is nearer to that external reality which is given to us, that concrete experience to which we are accustomed to ascribe exclusively truth; prophecy can but move in the terms supplied to a great extent by this very idealized history, as, for example, the Jewish expectations of the Messias King were an imaginative reproduction of the tradition of the Davidic kingdom. Yet it should be remembered that it is only when history has passed into prophecy that it affects the will, or tends to produce an active effort for better things; it is only when the Golden Age is thought of as a period which is to return, to be regained—it may be in more than pristine glory—that it becomes a source of joyful action or patience. In the hopes of Christ's second coming the primitive disciples did and suffered much; but how many Christians now-a-days abstain from marriage, or establish a community of goods, in the light of the speedy approach of their Master from heaven, and his millennial reign over the saints on earth? The majority either think, or act as though they thought, early Christian prophecy an illusion, even while they still think early Christian history a plain record of absolute fact. But the real distinction is sought for in the wrong place, and is not of the essential and permanent nature it is represented to be, when the Gospels are treated as the simplest and surest ground in the New Testament, and the Apocalypse as the most insecure and obscure. The very reverse is the true state of the case. The problem of the right general understanding of the Apocalypse is of far easier solution than the problem of the right understanding of the Gospels: it is easier to see into the ideal truth in the former than to disentangle the historical truth in the latter; for while the primary substance and starting point in the Gospels is, we will not say a series of external events, but at least an historical personality; the ultimate residuum in the Apocalypse is an idea, or set of ideas, more or less universal and omnipresent in the human mind; and the chief difficulty is, to put ourslves, by historical knowledge and criticism, in the right position to understand the particular form which these ideas assumed in Jewish Christendom. In the Gospels we have the idealization of the real and historical; in the Revelation we have the realization of the ideal represented in the forms present to the imagination of the writer; but to disentangle and abstract the historical person, the external reality, from the envelope or web in which it has been set, as in a shining garment, is a far more difficult task than to set free the ideal presented to us in the visions of the Apocalypse; for the ideal is present with us in one form or another through all generations, in our mind and heart; and we recognize easily the wants and wishes of the common spirit, even when it meets us in strange Eastern raiment.

What is here said is not, however, to be so understood as though the two processes of the imagination were severed from each other in act, or could not play upon the same objects at the same time. On the contrary; the most abstract and idealistic visions presuppose an historical reality, to which they have at once a negative and a positive relation; negatively they condemn it as insufficient for the ideal wants and happiness of man; positively they affirm it again, in the very fact of transforming and idealizing it into a state of happiness to come. And similarly the process of idealizing the actual is only possible in reference to given ideals and ideas; the historical fact or person can only be transfigured in accordance with the ideas of happiness or of perfection more or less consciously present in the mind of the artist, even though the artist be the common and sympathetic mind of a whole society. Thus in the works of imagination the relations between the real and the ideal shift through innumerable gradations; and now the one element, now the other obtains a preponderance, and the unity of their perfect balance is destroyed. In the gradual development of the Christian conception of the Person of Christ, we can see the ideal moment steadily gaining ground upon the strictly historical, and moulding the historical into conformity with itself. We see the process already carried a long way in the New Testament. With S. Paul, who had not known Christ after the flesh, *i.e.*, historically in life and outward experience, the Christ within is the highest and deepest truth, and the Christian life is the realization of this spiritual ideal in thought, word and deed. In the contrast between the Synoptic and the fourth Gospels we have a striking example of the results of the two methods; and it is hardly doubtful which of the two pictures of Christ is nearer the historical reality. Nevertheless the fourth Gospel has always been the favourite gospel of the deeper Christian consciousness, untroubled by the misgivings of over-scrupulous rationalism; and that, just because it is further from the historical truth, and nearer to the inner demand and satisfaction of ideal truth. The Synoptic Gospels, to be sure, are read by the devout Christian in the light of the fourth, or we may suspect that their difference from it would be more sensibly felt in general; and there is no doubt that a simple and unrationalizing faith in Christ, where such is still to be found, can only think of its Lord and Master as the perfect man, in every sense of that expression, with all the strength and all the beauty of character conceivable in man and woman. Such faith effects anew, in every generation, upon the traditional picture of Jesus the act of transfiguration in its own terminology according to its own contents. This act, which takes place in the hearts of believers, should reflect itself and find an abiding record, not merely in literature, but at least in painting too: and we might be tempted to take it as a sign of the feebleness and confusion of the inmost heart of Christendom in the present day, when we see the crude realism with which modern Art attempts the portraiture of the Son of Man. The ideal, or if we like to call it so, the supernatural, loses itself in a maze of external and arbitrary symbolism, none the less arbitrary because it is borrowed from real natural objects, or household utensils: and the historical and natural truth is reproduced, it may be, in an accurate portrait of a weak looking Syrian in strict Oriental surroundings; and instead of an "Ecce Homo," where the ideal may seem to have gained an expression within purely natural limits, and of a "Transfiguration" where the impossible is attempted in a form compatible with the serious belief of the time, and with the poetry of all time; we have a "Light of the World," or a "Shadow of the Cross," where the natural and the supernatural appear in mere juxta-position, held in one frame by a clever symbolism and a name, but in no wise fused into one by an inner and spiritual unity. If such pictures are the products and representatives of modern Christianity, its enemies might rejoice to think that it was degenerating into externals, incompatible with each other: but are they not rather witnesses to the state of orthodox and apologetic Theology, which in these days of cheap literature makes itself everywhere popular, with its half-and-half advances to criticism and concessions to rationalism, and its attempts to convert modern realism into an ally of dogmas which put an impassable gulf between nature and spirit?

For an elementary and unsophisticated consciousness as for the maturest reason, that dualism, which belongs to the intermediate stage of rationalistic inquiry—whether it be conducted in the interests of orthodoxy or of unorthodoxy—does not exist: the one may be said to be in a certain sense below it, the other above it; or, to avoid the appearance of a claim to moral superiority which might be attached to that mode of description, the one may be said to have this rationalistic dualism still before it, while the other can look back upon it as upon a necessary stage in the process of its own development. Thus reason restores the unity and fulness of the primitive intuition which has been disturbed and destroyed by the rationalism of the discursive understanding. This rationalism is represented in the present case by Church history, or that portion of it which is concerned with the systematization of dogma, and the dissolution of the same, effected chiefly by modern rationalism and science, since the Reformation. But in thus asserting its identity with the primitive consciousness, as well over against the theology of the modern Apologist, as over against the theology of the negative or sceptical Rationalist, critical philosophy asserts the identity with a difference: the whole process of thought during the centuries is not to go for nothing: and critical speculation claims a certain advantage over the primitive uncritical intuition in holding the truth without the illusion, or, what is the same thing, in recognizing the illusion as such; in semi-athanasian language there is an identity of substance (οὐσία) and a difference of form (πρόσωπον), or from a more modern standpoint, the objective reality is the same, though the temporary apprehension of it is different; the problem of thought is the same, though the terms of its solution be otherwise expressed. The illusive character of the primitive intuition consists in this, that it identifies the spiritual reality or ideal, of which it is immediately conscious, with what is after all a representation or symbol borrowed from the sensual world; or on the other hand, identifies the reality given in the sensible world as the vehicle of spiritual truth with this truth itself, and so in either case confuses together two spheres, the recognition of whose real difference is one of the last and most difficult steps in theoretic consciousness, though happily in practice Faith and Love find out a short way of their own.

The very terms in which we have here recognized the

illusive nature of primitive consciousness betray the difficulty of doing justice to the form in which that consciousness expressed itself. What is above written might easily be interpreted to mean that the identification of the spiritual and the sensual, of the eternal and the temporal, which is the secret of all claims to supernatural revelation, to absolute truth in dogmas, was the result in the first instance of a deliberate synthesis; that is not at all what is here intended. It is not until reflection has set in upon the given material, it is not until Theology, to speak roughly, has come to the aid or the injury of Religion, that the inconsistency of the various elements of the primitive faith or revelation, as doctrine, comes to light. And thus it conveys quite a false impression to speak of the Apostles as the "victims of illusion:" it is our doubts not our illusions which victimize us: and it is the intermediate stage between the original and naïve Realism of simple faith and the spiritual realism of a Reason at unity with itself, it is the stage of our theology and oppositions of science falsely so called, which is the period of our unhappiness. Joy, as has often been remarked, is one of the great characteristics of primitive Christendom; and so long and so far as that Joy is really one of the gifts of the Spirit, it indicates the unity of the Spirit with itself, it indicates the real presence of a spiritual truth.

We do not therefore say that the Apostles were free from what is to us illusion, on the contrary, a bitter experience was necessary before the illusion could be torn in twain; and it may be said perhaps of most Christians up to the present day, that the veil is on their hearts when they read Christian history or Christian prophecy: but we say that the illusion is not the chief thing, not the thing of permanent worth or practical importance, any more than of theoretical truth: it points to something below and above itself. Illusions too have their significance, and it is not accidental either that a man has just this illusion, or that it is just this man who has this illusion. To be a sharer in the bulk of the Messianic illusions, the notion of the thousand years reign, of the two resurrections, and so on, it was only necessary to be a Jew and a Pharisee; but to live in the specific illusion which differentiated the first Christians from their countrymen, it was necessary to have been with Jesus, and that too in more than the merely external sense. Whether it be the Master who chooses his disciples, or the disciples who choose their Master, the relation points to an internal compatibility and correspondence, to some "elective affinity;" and the men whom Jesus called his friends cannot have been quite unworthy of his friendship. And as the Messianic expectations of the Jewish people, however illusive—and the theologian most dead in dogmatic presuppositions will allow that *the Jews* were filled with illusive hopes and expectations—point nevertheless to a grand and ideal truth of which the whole people was possessed; so the concentration of all these hopes and beliefs on Jesus, the identification of Jesus with the Messias by his immediate followers, points to the fact that he in his person answered their ideal, and justified in their minds the claim which he perhaps made. In a far higher degree is the impression which Jesus had made upon them during his life established in its ideal proportions, when we suppose that the visions which the Apostles had of their Master after his death were the results, not of external supernatural interposition, but of the internal working of their own hearts and minds.

By no slight impact could such "convulsions of the soul" have been produced. The visions which testify to the earnestness and genuineness of the Disciples, testify, in an even greater degree to the spiritual impression which the lost Master must have made upon them, while he was still with them.

The visions themselves were no illusions; the illusion lay in the explanation of the visions; and the explanation could only be couched in the current forms of the time and place. But it may now fairly be said that just in proportion as we recognize the visions as natural products, so must the natural cause assume larger proportions, so must the historical Person of Christ grow in importance, even if it be at the expense of the sacrifice of one more illusion. And so from the ground of history and criticism the Person of Christ gains not loses by the transfiguration which it underwent, and in which it manifested itself to his disciples. In reconstructing the life and person of Jesus of Nazareth we stand upon a solid ground of history, and know that the materials offered have some value, direct or indirect; and the belief in his Resurrection is not the least but perhaps the greatest of the indirect proofs of his veritable exaltation above the common level of humanity during his life on earth.

To effect this reconstruction is the task and pure interest of historical science when directed to the origin of Christianity; and from the importance which seems to accrue to the Person of Christ from the fearless application of critical methods to the material for reconstructing his life, it might seem for an instant as though the results of criticism could only be acceptable to the inherited dogma of the divinity of that Person. It is indeed not improbable that the naïve tactics of the Apologist will repeat themselves in this instance also. The history of religion and of theology shows that it is a law of progress here that the primary identification of the Finite with the Infinite, of the temporal with the eternal, should yield to critical analysis in one point, only to reassert itself more clearly and expressly in another: so it was at the Reformation, where the divine authority of the given Book took the place of the divine authority of the Church; so it is now with the more progressive Theologians, who are ready to give up the Book to the ordinary processes of Criticism, if they may keep the supernatural and authoritative event intact. There is a step further to be taken; the event too may be given up; some wondrous theory may be excogitated to bring the pre-existent Deity into special relation with the created man; and the whole argument of Critic and Apologist may concentrate itself round the Person of Christ.

That Christian Theology would thus gain very much by concentration on its proper problem—viz., the elucidation of "the mind which was in Christ Jesus," the determination of the fundamental elements of that consciousness which has been the source of such life and strength to humanity, spite of all the errors, superstitions, or illusions through which it has made its way in the world—is not doubtful. And this was indeed always the chief interest of Christendom, at least until the Roman Church and the development of Papal claims usurped the place belonging of right to the Person of Christ. The Athanasian Creed itself is the result of the controversy as to the nature of Christ; and the doctrine of the Trinity has developed in accordance with the needs of the Christology. Protestantism, (which in its best heart is the protest against every human or finite power which sets itself in the place of God, or identifies itself with the sole divine authority, and consequently on its positive side the appeal from man to God,) restored the supreme interest in the Person of Christ. Certainly our Protestantism did not at once see the full application of its own implicit principle, and in its protest against the finite authority of the Church, itself identified the Bible with the absolute and final authority : but it only requires time for this identification also to be given up. Already the Christian Theologian is falling back upon a supernatural phenomenon as the key to the divine Revelation; a few years more, and we may see this too abandoned, and all stress laid upon a divine Person. But the inner contradiction is still there, and will remorselessly demand the sacrifice of this illusion as of its predecessors, and the complete freedom of the divine and final authority from all conditions of time and space. It will then seem a sort of heathenism to identify Jesus with God : it will then seem a necessity to distinguish the Divine Principle even from the Person in whom it may first have become manifest; it will then seem possible to realize the divine Sonship and heritage, without transferring the metaphor into the abstract regions of a transcendental Godhead, and reproducing it again as a verity above and beyond human reason, to be accepted in spite of self-contradiction as a divine revelation.

The identification of the finite with the infinite, even in its highest form, viz., the identification of Jesus with God, must necessarily contain this inner contradiction; not merely because every finite existence is in its time and place a manifestation of the Absolute Being, which cannot therefore be exhausted in any one manifestation; but because the eternal is *ex hypothesi* different in kind from the temporal, which is nevertheless here identified with it. This is the error of Heathendom as a Religion, whether polytheistic or pantheistic, to identify the temporal and phenomenal appearance with the eternal principle of which it might be the manifestation. On the other hand, the opposite theory, which in order to avoid this pantheistic identification abstracts the infinite from the finite, and establishes a dualistic antinomy between them, involves a self-contradiction no less fatal; for the abstract infinite is conceived still in a form borrowed from the finite, as a Person, an infinite or absolute Person, which, it is confessed, is a *contradictio in adjecto*.

This contradiction in the idea of God is really rendered necessary by the contradiction in the dogma of Christ's Deity; logically indeed the former is a presupposition for the latter; but historically the development of the latter has led the way, and determined the shape to be taken by the former. Once given the antithesis of the finite and the infinite, and given their unity in the Person of Christ, as an object for the speculative theologian, there were two rocks upon which the given dogma might suffer shipwreck: those who laid most stress upon the transcendental nature of the Infinite, tended to fall into an abstract Deism on the one side, and on the other, to reduce Christ to the level of ordinary humanity, or at least to represent him as an inferior, even if angelic, being. Those who laid most stress upon the reality of the Divinity in Christ, were inclined to eliminate the human or finite element altogether, and fall into speculations of a pantheistic character. In the development and explication of her dogma the Church pursued the *via media* of asserting both extremes at once beside each other as alike true, however contradictory; and the Athanasian Creed remains as the faithful witness and result of this procedure, and the logical development of the dogma which was the starting point of the whole process: ὁ λόγος σὰρξ ἐγένετο (the Word was made flesh. John i. 14).

But this re-assertion is no solution; both members of the contradiction remain beside and outside each other, each plainly false in its especial one-sidedness, and each justified in its one-sidedness as against the other. If Christ is God, he is not man : if man, not God. If God is absolute, he is not a Person : if a Person, not absolute. The difficulty is not any the less striking when it is transferred to the supposed inner relations of the Godhead itself; if there are three Persons, and each is God, there are three Gods; if there is but one God, there are not three Persons, in our sense of the word.

It was not written in heaven that these hopeless problems should be solved upon the path of theological controversy; there was need of a fresh polemic, not between theologian and theologian, but between theologian and secular science, before the right standpoint for their abolition or absorption could develop itself. Whatever may be the errors of men of science in their special realms, the pursuit and acquisition of natural knowledge implies a set of presuppositions and conditions utterly incompatible with the presupposition of dogmatic theology : the key to the scientific position, the condition on which alone science is possible, may be variously expressed, but it remains under various expressions fundamentally the same, be it named, the uniformity of nature, or the continuity of experience, or the trust that God will work in such a way as not to put us to permanent intellectual confusion. This is certainly a metaphysical principle ; and it may very well be the case, that men devoted to special inquiries do not perceive the full bearing and significance of the principle upon which they work, explicitly or implicitly: it is not necessary for the special sciences that they should, any more than for ordinary everyday life and experience, which also implies, as is seen upon analysis, exactly the same principle. But this principle of unity, this metaphysical monism, once recognized as the only possible theoretic and practical "view of the whole universe, of all being and of all life," must work an end to the absolute dualism, which is the theoretic presupposition of supernaturalism, for the latter implies a contradiction in the ultimate being of things, before which nothing awaits us but permanent intellectual confusion.

To the antithesis which made itself good in the idea of God (and which led to Deism or Pantheism, according as one or other member of the contradiction was raised to sole validity), corresponds in the idea of Nature the antithesis of matter and mind; and the same process of one-sided assertion repeats itself here, with the same final solution, which is no solution. It is indeed an involuntary witness to the rational necessity of a metaphysical monism that the whole explanation of the world is now given from the side of materialism alone, now from the side of idealism alone. Even in their extremest forms each must be allowed a certain right over against the other; and neither consequently can be recognized as final or satisfactory. On the one hand we must admit that every existence is ideal, inasmuch as it comes to us only as and in an act of consciousness; and the whole world appears to be a creation of our own minds. On the other hand, we cannot deny that we are ourselves members of the world, creatures of nature, results of material processes, of processes independent of ourselves, and all our ideas and volitions; and so it might seem as though the ideal moment in existence were only a product and function of the material. We are thus involved in a circle, in a contradiction: matter is but an idea; and yet the idea, the state of consciousness, presupposes matter. Some of those who perceive the dilemma think to come straight out of it by asserting both members of it to be equally justified in their claims; others, by representing the whole discussion as a mere quarrel about words. But even a quarrel about words is instructive; and as in one sense all discussion whatever is a quarrel about words, we are not helped much further by such a merely negative criticism. To reassert both idealism and materialism in the same breath as equally right is no solution of the difficulty; it is but its recognition; though as such, it is not without its value.

Just as the dualistic contradiction in our Theology started from the Christology and its given dogma, ὁ λόγος σὰρξ ἐγένετο (the Word was made flesh): so the dualism in our modern philosophy dates from Descartes, and his celebrated anthropological word; *Cogito, ergo sum* (thinking proves existence). Given this word as the starting-point, the progress of metaphysics exhibited, just as the progress of theology had done, the continued separation and driving out of one another of the two elements originally set in juxta-position, now the exclusive assertion of the one, now the exclusive assertion of the other, and now their attempted re-union by means of a third, which in its turn must fall into the same elementary antithesis, or finally, their bare re-assertion one beside the other. It is the abiding merit of Kant to have opened the door to the true solution of the metaphysical problem; negatively, by having shown the refutation as well of Materialism and of Idealism, as of the dogmatic combination of both; positively, by having given a new starting-point and firmament for metaphysical thought, in the denial of transcendental knowledge of any kind, and the assertion of the legitimacy of experience, or if we may so say, the reality of natural knowledge. This is exactly the same thing as saying that the only legitimate metaphysics must be monistic: that this should again be misunderstood, and that the post-Kantian philosophy should again fall into the old antithesis of abstract Idealism and abstract Materialism, was not without an excuse in Kant himself. For Kant only went half-way in his negation; and from such a negation only a half-position could be won. He denied transcendental knowledge, but left transcendental existence as a problem on the limits of Reason: and so he did not clear himself of the wreck and fragments of Dualism. The world of knowledge is one thing, and there is, after all—to this the Kantian doctrine of the "Ding an sich" virtually comes—a transcendental world, behind or above. Such an admission or postulate is a permanent challenge to the human mind to overreach itself; for it must always appear purely arbitrary that the Reason should be entitled and indeed compelled to make a purely existential proposition, that "God is," for example; and have absolutely no ground to go on to qualify this assertion by saying What God is. The arbitrariness of the Kantian postulate is aggravated when it is seen that this transcendental Thing is historically a survival of the old Dogmatism, or a concession to it, which has no theoretic value; and indeed it is not till Kant comes to practice that he assigns anything but a negative value to the transcendental postulates. But it is not till we see that theoretically speaking the "Ding an sich" is a piece of abstract realism, is, that is to say, an abstraction taken from the world of space and time and given a reality which is purely imaginary, that we have courage not merely to deny its cognoscibility, but also its existence.

But this denial of another world (as a metaphysical reality) would remain a mere negation, if we could not explain how it ever comes to be asserted. And this explanation can only be given when we have gained a clear insight into the nature and methods of thought, and how it is that we come by the contents of our consciousness at all. The logical starting-point for all knowledge is the Socratic axiom, γνῶθι σεαυτόν (know thyself): upon the right distinction of the elements of our own nature from one another depends our insight into the nature of the ultimate metaphysical categories or first principles, which render knowledge and existence possible. The science of the soul is the propædeutic to all other science, whether physical or metaphysical.

Consciousness is a web woven of stuff supplied to us by an external world; and this externality, however we may name it, is as necessary a datum of consciousness as the self of which we are said to have most immediate cognition. But the external world as presented to us is not a chaos; it is already an order of nature; there is method and reason in it, in virtue of which alone are we, as rational beings, enabled to appropriate the experience which comes to us. That this external order, or ideal unity of things, is omnipresent, is indeed a late discovery for scientific consciousness; but omnipresent unity is implied in knowledge and potentially contained in it from the very first. Practically speaking, however, experience comes to us in the first instance as perception through the senses, and it is only as thought that it becomes for us science, a system, and loses its accidental character by the discovery or recognition of the inherent order, to a belief in which order we have committed ourselves in our first act of knowledge. Thus the goal of all scientific endeavour is the gradual conversion of sensual experience (whether dependent or independent of human volition) into a necessary order of ideas for consciousness; or, in other words, the gradual identification of our explicit consciousness with the reason inherent in things, the realization in our minds of the world, which came to us first as a vague multiplicity of objects (or of sensations), as a rational whole or unity, as a universe.

The psychological process, by which the *carte blanche* of man's mind is being filled in with knowledge, is the formation, by abstraction and generalization, of ideas applicable to many objects, but not indissolubly associated with any special object; from these ideas are formed more abstract and general notions, still further removed from the fulness of the individual perceptions of definite external objects. These general notions, being on the one hand products and contents of the mind, have a spiritual or intellectual character, they are ideas; being on the other hand only more or less blurred and attenuated copies of sensible things, they never quite lose the properties which are indissoluble from time and space, they always remain ideas of sense, sensations in the abstract, symbols of possible sensations; they have not a purely and completely ideal character.

But in the hunt for Truth, what has been sought and implied as a presupposition from the first in the process of consciousness, is the pure rationality of the world. The mind has contained this presupposition, even at the very outset, but as an empty form, a naked idea, a potentiality, to be filled up and clothed upon, and raised by experience to actual knowledge. Now on the way to its goal, the filling in of this formal unity with material contents by means of experience (or as it may be otherwise expressed, the establishment of a balance or equation between its own ideal unity and the multiplicity of external objects and events, all relative to that unity), the mind encounters those abstract sensations above described, takes them for the ideal world it is looking for, and expects to find in one of them, in the most abstract of them, the full unity and complete truth of thought; identifies, that is, the first principles of things, the fundamental unity or unities of concrete reality, with the most abstract ideas of sensation which it can form at the time being. The mind represents to itself the pure ideas of the Reason, God, the Soul, the World, when it seeks to realize their truth, under the form of this or that abstract of sensations; not unnaturally so, for these notions, abstracted from sensation, form as it were a world of *quasi* ideas between the inner unity of the subject or self, and the outer unity of the object or not-self; and as it is the sensibility and not the rationality, the material and not the ideal moment of external existence which forces itself first upon the mind, the reality of a being, even *ex hypothesi* spiritual, admits of being represented to the mind at first only under the forms of sensible existence.

Abstract ideas are each of them the ideal unity of a mass of sensations, and are in so far powers for systematizing experience; but when used by the mind as equivalent to absolute ideal unities, which cannot be subject to time and space, and the contradictions which belong to temporal and spatial existence, they collapse; for their intrinsic materiality, their inheritance of sensation, makes itself apparent as a contradiction of the ideal unity postulated, and refuses to be reduced to rest or self-identity. From the very first they have consisted of two heterogeneous elements, the element of indefinite multiplicity or sensation, and the element of unity or form, which is purely rational; and when such a complex compound is taken as absolute unity, as the real form of pure spirit, it falls to pieces in the contradiction between the absolute unity which is sought and the relative unity which has been identified with it; and the development and explication of this contradiction produces a dialectical process in the history of human thought between the antitheses of Dogmatism and Scepticism, Materialism and Idealism, Supernaturalism and Rationalism, which can never find a satisfactory termination so long as the dispute is carried on without a critical discrimination of the fundamental metaphysical difference between Spirit in time and in eternity.

The Soul has been sent out to seek and find itself and the spiritual unity outside itself which is implied in its own derivative or created unity, and which it desires to assimilate; and now believes itself to have arrived at the goal, when it catches at a self-representation under the form of abstract sensation, the form for example abstracted from the human body as seen in the phenomenal world. But what the soul is seeking is some purely spiritual being, and this form is not purely spiritual, but on the one hand has a material element, for it is borrowed from sense; and on the other hand has not even material reality, for it is but an abstract notion. Therefore, the very contradiction arises here in the idea of the Soul, which belongs to any notion of an absolute thing (Ding an sich), and which we have already recognized in the notion of God as an absolute Person: for all things or persons are essentially relative existences. Never can the soul come to itself so long as it represents its own spiritual essence under the forms of sensible existence; for every such existence, every thing, always exhibits the two moments, the ideal and the material, and so the search is everlasting, or ends in the sceptical recognition of ultimate antinomies, so long as the unity which is postulated as eternal is still represented under similitudes borrowed from space and time.

Thus in considering the three metaphysical realities, God, the Soul, and the World, we are necessarily involved in endless contradiction so long as we conceive their mode of being as analogous to the existence of sensible things and individuals; for the implicit postulate from which we start in the consideration of these absolute spiritual unities is that they are other and different to the visible creation. That we should involve ourselves in the dialectical process provoked by such self-contradictory conceptions may be a result of the nature and limitation of our mental faculties, and the consequent necessity for a gradual development of science from a naïve and uncritical state to fuller consciousness of self and other. At least, it may fairly be said of the metaphysicians that they have not been so wrong-headed as might seem at first sight. They have been less blind or dull to the conditions of any knowledge at all than those who, because a hundred systems have had their day and ceased to be, conclude that the metaphysical element in knowledge is delusive or transitory. All knowledge and experience contain such an element, and it is just this ingredient which gives stability and certainty to the whole, and lifts it clear of the changes and chances of mere mortality. A science of Fore- and After- Physics is implied in the existence of physical science itself, which gives no account of its own first principles and assumptions; that this knowledge other than the bare and empirical knowledge of sensible things should be taken for knowledge of another world pre-existent and post-existent, is an indiscriminate confusion of things temporal and things eternal, a conversion of metaphor into metaphysics, which is inevitable to a certain stage in the development of thought, owing to the method by which the human Reason proceeds in the formation of its ideas, and the recognition of truth. All knowledge as such is ideal, the crassest materialism only exists by a virtue not its own, inasmuch as the sensible experience or the external world, which it proclaims as the Alpha and Omega of science, is assumed to be an organized and systematic, that is, a rational and ideal whole. In general, people, even of a philosophic turn, find it easier to admit the spiritual reality of God and of the Soul than that of the World, and find themselves tempted to think of the spiritual world as removed in time and place from the material. In other words, it is harder to think of the "System of Nature" as spiritual, not material; it is harder to realize the ideal of Nature as a spiritual reality, and not merely an abstraction, not merely a notion derived from experience, than to envisage the idea of God or of the Soul; yet at the very same time the spiritual world is more hopelessly identified with a world of time and space, of matter and sense, over again, than are the two other rational ideas. But this false abstraction, whereby the spiritual unity or substance of the world is represented as after all matter, but matter removed in time and space from the matter of the visible universe, involves a similar false abstraction in the mode of conceiving God and the Soul: the absolute Spirit, whose habitation is the spiritual world, is conceived of after the likeness and similitude of *a* man, *i.e.* as one individual among other individuals, a person with other persons beside him: and the Soul or finite Spirit is conceived of, if not as an ætherial body, at least as a material force, or a second substance within, even if independent of the individual body to which it is allied, to which it is tied and bound, in which it is incarcerated, or however else the accidental conjunction of two separate substances may be expressed in the terms of the dualistic theory which underlies the orthodox and popular terminology on these matters.

If the individual soul were of the nature thus ascribed to it, could it be a matter of indifference or obscurity what becomes of any particular soul at its separation from the body? The spiritualism of our day, which reposes on the same crude psychological and metaphysical dualism as the current theology, gives the answer of the natural man to this question. Turning to Revelation from the standpoint of such a theory it cannot but appear a matter of considerable importance, specially with reference to the doctrine of the Resurrection, to determine what is the fate of the soul immediately on its separation from the body, or whether the soul can exist at all without a body material, and if so, in what condition. For the solution of such questions by a Christian in the light of the great principle of Christianity set by Dr. Westcott at the head of his chapter, treating of the bearings of the Resurrection of Christ on the individual Christian, it might be thought that the Church doctrine as to the fate of Christ's Soul during the three days which intervened between its separation from the body on the Cross and its reunion with the same in the Sepulchre, would be of considerable significance. But this is just one of the points where the doctrines of the Church and the Bible stand in clearest divergence from and antithesis to the present teaching of science; also, fortunately, where the practical Christian life has glided beyond the storm of controversy, and is to a great extent independent of the dogma as theory; and so, albeit no one would deny that on the principle above alluded to, a flood of light would be thrown not merely on the destiny but on the nature of the soul, could we know what became of the soul of Jesus during the interval between his death and resurrection;*

* The Descent into Hell was not indeed in any of the early *Creeds*, even as preserved by Augustin; but for all that he says: " Quis nisi infidelis negaverit fuisse apud inferos Christum ?" It may originally, as Bishop Pearson says, have been equivalent in the Creeds, where it was introduced without further explicit reference to the Burial, merely to an assertion that Christ's Body was buried; in which case it is another instance of the gradual development of legendary details, and just as the Resurrection was quickly differentiated by a materializing phantasy into Resurrection and Ascension, so Burial was multiplied into Burial and Descent into Hell. This multiplication was effected in popular Christian Belief long before it found its expression in the Creeds; and in spite of Bishop Pearson the more probable interpretation of 1 Peter iii. 18, 19, is the more materialistic. The article ($\tau\hat{\omega}$ $\pi\nu\epsilon\acute{\upsilon}\mu\alpha\tau\iota$) which is important for his interpretation, though not conclusive, is a doubtful reading. The Gospel of Nicodemus gives a detailed account of the circumstances attendant on the Descent and sojourn in the Shades, as narrated by Charinus and Lenthius, the sons of Simeon, who were permitted to rise, remain on earth for three days, make written depositions before the high priests, after which "they were changed into exceeding white forms, and were seen no more." This represents the early popular imaginations on the subject; which reappear also in mediæval art, in pictures of the deliverance, etc., of the souls in prison on the advent of Christ in Hades.

it is easier and more discreet for the modern Apologist to pass over the question as lightly as possible; not because there is no primitive teaching on this head, but because such teaching is in more flagrant opposition to modern science than admits of serious defence.

The dictum of modern science is that a soul cannot

Bishop Pearson is sceptical as to the details of the Descent and Return; but he acknowledges that there was a local downward motion of the soul of Jesus in separation from his body. The belief that Christ raised with him from Hades a number of the Old Testament saints, is supported by Matt. xxvii. 52, 53. (Patriarchæ et prophetæ appendices dominicæ resurrectionis. Tertullian, cit. in C. L. Müller, op. cit. § 10.) There was also a less material idea; *e.g.*, Gregory of Nyssa thinks not of a place but a state— καταστάσιν τινὰ τῆς λογικῆς φύσεως διὰ θανάτου τῶν σαρκικῶν ἀπολελυμένην ὅπερ ἐν ψυχαῖς θεωρεῖται, quoted in Müller, § 8. But this spiritualism is as foreign to orthodox mediæval as to native Jewish belief. Before Christ, Abraham was in hell; after Christ, the crucified thief was in Paradise. Alger, op. cit. p. 227, quoting Jerome. Cp. 1 Peter iii. 19 f., iv. 6; Luke xxiii. 43, xvi. 22 ff. Paul's belief on this point also may very well have been more refined than that of the Brethren in Jerusalem. Cp. 1 Thess. iv. 14-17; Phil. i. 23. Professor Westcott seems to doubt the conscious existence of the soul apart from the body, p. 146: "There is no reason to suppose that the soul separated from the body is personal." He sees rightly enough that on rational principles there is as much to be said for the Pre- as for the Post-existence of the individual soul. All the more obscure for him, "the intermediate state of the soul after death and before the Resurrection;" and he prudently says nothing about it except that "probably there is something wholly deceptive in our use of words of time ('before' and 'after') in such a connexion." A remark to which we may heartily assent, and only press for its fearless application. The Descent into Hell, however, in its material signification is an integral and consistent development and part of the belief in material Resurrection; and should not be so lightly passed over, if, at least, it is one of the great principles of Christianity that all which happened to Jesus Christ is to take place in the soul and in the body of each Christian.

exist without a body: so, those who wish to reconcile the dogma that the soul exists after death with this dictum, are driven to some hypothesis which may smooth away the uncompromising dualism of the old dogma. Hence the spectacle of the latest apologetic attempt to find new bottles for old wine, which represents the soul as the architect of its own "spiritual body" during this life, by action upon who knows how many intervening orders of æther rings, till at death the soul (hitherto quite unconscious apparently of this unseen building) finds a fresh vessel equipped for a further voyage after this body of death has gone under. A perusal of "The Unseen Universe" can leave no doubt on the mind that this apology is not an intentional *reductio ad absurdum* of the doctrine which it professes to defend, nor is it merely an essay in the poetry of science, though much therein contained lends itself readily to a poetical supernaturalism, which must have a charm for all but pedantic dogmatists: the attempt made is made in sober honesty. None the less must we marvel at the reception which the work has found from some orthodox reviews; that they should allow the apologetic intention of the book to blind them to its real bearings on orthodox doctrine must be written down to the "destiny which shapes our ends rough hew them how we will." That the doctrine put forward in this book of the gradual formation of a body by the action of the soul itself upon invisible matter—for the unseen universe is still material—to be a vehicle for the soul at its departure from the visible body—death being as it were the junction where the spiritual passenger changes carriages—could be confounded either with the ordinary Christian doctrine of the Resurrection of the body on the one hand, or with the Pauline doctrine of a "spiritual body" on the other;

seems to show the ignorance or the desperation of everyday Apologetics. The new argument for the survival of the soul, based upon the hypothetical possibility of its construction for itself of an invisible body independent of the visible body, is fatal to the orthodox doctrine of the Resurrection of the Body, or of the Flesh as it is sometimes even put, just in proportion as it is strong for the immortality of the Soul; and instead of a general resuscitation and resurrection at the last day, we have at best the change in each individual consciousness at death produced by the discovery that it is in possession of an ætherial (but still material) organism, of which hitherto it knew nothing. Further, between the æther body of the authors of "The Unseen Universe" and the spiritual body of S. Paul there is at first sight, taking each in isolation from the separate systems in which they severally find suitable place, a possible identification: but when we consider the respective sources and relations of the two notions, their coherence disappears. The spiritual body of the Epistle to the Corinthians is indeed composed of a celestial matter, but it is composed in a moment, in the twinkling of an eye, at the last trump, it is a miraculous work: it is of matter not invisible to eyes miraculously opened, but of matter supernatural and different in kind from matter terrestrial: and the notion in this case hangs together with a theory respecting the material earth and heavens, their laws and difference of substance, which has been abolished and replaced by the Copernican system, the Law of Gravitation, and the results of the Spectrum analysis. The spiritual body in "The Unseen Universe" is the fair result of an incoherent synthesis of modern physics and ancient theology.* It is not super-

* The theological orthodoxy of men of science may be expected

natural, of miraculous fiat, but developed gradually during this life by the action of the human soul itself in conformity with natural laws and the principle of continuity. Whatever may be the worth of this hypothetical body tested by the canons or conclusions of metaphysics, it is in itself, and in the set of presuppositions which it implies, as far from identity with the Pauline notion of a spiritual body, as the indifference of the theory of Christ's Person to the question of his Resurrection and our immortality, professed by these authorities, is from the apostolic gospel of faith in a crucified and glorified Messias.

"If Christ rose from the dead, immortality becomes more than possible; it becomes probable; and we do not see that this conclusion is greatly modified by differences in our mode of regarding the exact nature of Christ."* The chief interest which animates the last attempt to rescue the bare dogma of the Resurrection of Jesus, apparently is the belief in personal immortality, which is supposed to be rendered probable if he rose from the dead. That this is not the case has been already pointed out; least of all could it be the case irrespective of our view of the nature of Christ; nor shall we be assisted to really probable conclusions in one of two allied lines by inexactness in the other. On scientific principles we could only conclude that given the Resurrection of Jesus as an historical event, wherever the same spiritual and material forces were again united under similar circumstances, the same event would be effected. To spring

---

to vary (*cæteris paribus*), concomitantly with the anthropological bearings of their studies. Chemists will be more unorthodox than pure physicists or mathematicians, biologists than chemists, and so on.

* "The Unseen Universe," p. 199, 1st Ed. (p. 256, 6th Ed.)

from the particular fact of the Resurrection of Jesus to the general doctrine of the Immortality of the Human Soul, and that too irrespective of our mode of regarding the nature of Jesus, seems a saltus rather startling to any one imbued, be it ever so little, with a spirit of logical continuity. It would seem a more scientific procedure to attempt to show the immortality of the soul by an examination of its own nature and conditions of existence than by appeal to a past event of a most exceptional character on any theory. The Resurrection of Christ in any case would not be of much service without the complementary fact of his Ascension; for he might have risen from the dead once and returned to them again a second time and permanently : but of the second event we read nothing in "The Unseen Universe," though it surely has if anything a more direct intimation of Immortality than the first.

The great interest which concentrates itself in modern theology upon the doctrine of a future personal immortality;—insomuch that the old Creed in its entirety seems often to be maintained for the sake of this one dogma which is thought to be interwoven with it, or supported and substantiated by it;—offers a great contrast to the religion of the Bible, whether in the Old or New Testament. In the New Testament many expressions are to be found which look, especially when read from a modern standpoint, as if the chief moment in the Christian Revelation were an endless life after death for the individual in bliss : but set in their proper perspective such expressions will be seen to be anything but dogmatic statements about a life to come in another world. The Messianic expectations of primitive Christendom can scarcely be identified with the hope of personal immortality; and we may indeed say that the Eschatology of the first Christians—if we may use a theological term for what was still rather imaginative belief than a technical formula—making as it did so much of the community, so little comparatively of the individual (where the Church not the Soul was the Bride of Christ), though expressed in forms which may now appear illusive, reveals in this respect perhaps a grander spirit than does the preoccupation with his own personal prospects which is not seldom the source of faith in a modern Christian. If the original individuality of Paul, and his dissent from the Church in Jerusalem might have tended to make him anxious for the doctrine of the personal future life of the individual; his strong practical faith, his missionary zeal, and not least his sense of the mystical union of the believer with Christ, secured with him the supreme interest for the new life in the present; he too speaks at times of the Resurrection as though it had already taken place, and he too proclaims that principle of the solidarity of the Church, of all men that is potentially, which is one of the surest springs of a large humanity. Still more predominant is the thought not of future but of present immortal life in the Johannine writings, wherein the doctrine of death and resurrection and new life in Christ is still further and more explicitly developed. The best minds of the New Testament, we may fairly say, do not ignore the doctrine of a future life for the individual; but are very far from making it in its abstraction the pearl of revelation, or the cause and motive of righteousness and newness of life. And what is said of the New Testament may be said quite as emphatically of the Old. Few theologians will now venture to say that the Old Testament does not preserve for us the highest utterances of religious inspiration before

Christ; yet so weak and indistinct are the traces of any definite doctrine of personal immortality in the Old Testament that its absence has been made the ground of an assertion that the Old Testament contains no revelation at all by those who thought this doctrine essential to all Religion.* And certainly if the Old Testament revelation had been designed to make known a personal immortality as now conceived, it failed very conspicuously of its purpose; and we see even in the New Testament to what straits the Jews of the days of Jesus were driven in their attempts to read into the sacred books from the first the doctrine of Resurrection or even that of immortality.† But in truth, as has well been said, we might take it as a proof of the sublimity of the revelation preserved in the Old Testament, that it contains, not a doctrine of future immortality, but a series of protests more or less explicit against the doctrine of immortality in all the forms then current in the world, from the simple naturalism of Shamanism to the elaborate morality of Persian dualism.‡ This is its negative service to humanity, just as its posi-

* *E.g.*, in the fourth Wolfenbüttler Fragment ("Dass die Bücher A. T. nicht geschrieben worden, eine Religion zu offenbaren"). So too Kant, in the "Religion innerhalb der Grenzen der reinen Vernunft."

† *E.g.*, in the argument put into Jesus' mouth against the Sadducees to prove the Resurrection—an argument which could not even prove a Life to come, on any acceptable principles of evidence. Matt. xxii. 23 ff.; Mark xii. 18 ff.; Luke xx. 27 ff. The Synoptists however may be supposed to have thought it a crushing reply—so it was, perhaps, on Rabbinical principles of interpretation.

‡ This is admirably brought out in a small work entitled: "Das negative Verdienst des Alten Testaments um die Unsterblichkeits-Lehre, dargestellt von Dr. Hermann Engelbert," Berlin, 1857, though perhaps some of the details are a little too methodically carried out.

tive desert is to have maintained at all costs the assertion of the righteousness, mercy, and truth of God. The Old Testament is no less fatal to every form of pessimism and nihilism; but our minds are so much preoccupied by the introspective habits of the latter centuries, and we are so deeply prejudiced in favour of the opinion that our own existence is the chief if not the only certainty, that not a little of modern religion is, theoretically viewed, not much removed from the teaching of that Indian school of interpreters, who hold the world an illusion, and deny the eternity of God, but recognize after a fashion the future life of the individual souls of men.*

Such has never been the prevalent colour of Western thought; and our common sense and the current philosophy of language recognize fully the reality of the ideas which we have been considering, whatever disputes be waged in the schools as to their natures severally. But in nearly all discourse, whether popular or esoteric, the same presumption reigns, that the spiritual object which is sought exists in the form of a sensible object, that the reality which is the ground of phenomena is itself a phenomenon. This mode of conceiving spiritual truth, as it involves the antinomies which we have noticed, so it causes that what are but different moments, sides, aspects, elements, or however they be called, of one

* The notion of a spiritual Body is found in the Vedas; and in the Sânkhya system of interpretation is combined with Atheism, and the notion of a multiplicity of individual souls, pre- and post-existent, *i.e.*, practically immortal. Each soul has a primitive Body, consisting of nineteen out of the twenty-four elements, inseparable from it through all its wanderings: at birth it receives as well a material body of the five coarser elements (Æther, Air, Light, Water, Earth) from the parents.—Wurm: " Geschichte der indischen Religionen," pp. 119 ff.

spiritual object in permanence, are thought and spoken of as different periods, stages or states removed from each other in space and time. Such is, for example, in the case of God, the assertion of an act of creation before which there was nothing, standing as it does in opposition to the unchangeableness of the divine nature: such too are all modes of speaking of God which predicate psychological alteration of him. The same mode of thought is exemplified with reference to the World, when the spiritual side of creation is spoken of as another world removed in time and place from the present; or when the good in the world is regarded as an ideal age in its history past or future. Of this character too are all modes of thinking of the Soul which transform internal psychological relations into external temporal events or changes; making, for example, its original sin an inheritance from an external and so far accidental event in the life of the first Adam, and its eternal and intrinsic bliss or woe as external a result of its relation to the second.

Such are the modes of popular thought; and upon the same level, in dogmatic theology (which has formularized the popular thought into a logical system and then identified this system with the truth contained in the popular religious intuition on the one side and with scientific truth on the other), the battle of Faith comes to be identified with the triumph of a way of thinking, to wit, its own way. That this way is full of contradictions is no objection in the eyes of the theologian, who closes every path of ratiocination with the dead wall of a "Credo quia absurdum:" and in a certain fashion he is right. A spiritual truth expressed in sensible forms involves, as we have said, a contradiction; and the more adequate and full the expression is, on the given level, the more manifest and explicit will be the contradiction; but for this very reason, on the given level, it is not any rationalistic or semi-rationalistic attempts to mitigate the apparent harshness of orthodox dogma which keep us nearest the truth; and in the dialectic process of the development of doctrine we throw in our lot with the Church rather than with the heretics. But we must not for all that fall into the error of the theologians, and confuse Faith as a saving grace with a particular way of thinking of the Trinity or of the Unity. It is the doom of nearly all theologians, whether Christian or other, seeing rightly enough that there can be no religion without dogmas in one sense, to identify Faith with the theoretical tradition which has come down to them, however far it may be from anything which the believer can now comprehend or apprehend in his own experience, or even by analogy from the experience of others. But this is hardly the biblical meaning of the term, and upon the Bible we may fall back as on the most authoritative code and chronicle of religious insight and experience. If there ever was a writer who from the vigour and depth of his dialectical gifts and interest might have been betrayed into identifying Faith with a particular mode of thought, or a particular set of views, it was surely S. Paul; yet had he given Faith such a meaning he could hardly have spoken of the Faith of Abraham as though it were not essentially different from his own; nor can the Faith which is set beside Hope and Charity, even though less than Charity, be a thing so little as any particular mode of thought. But it is a danger which attends much thinking about God that we may come to confound our Creed with our Faith, or even "the Faith;" and a writer so liberal and tender as

Dr. Westcott can fall into the error (apparently) of speaking as though "the victory of Faith" to be wrought nowadays were the victory of one way of thinking over another, of one view of the universe, &c., or, as if there were one theoretic view of these objects handed down to us, which could be taken as *the* truth in the religious sense of the word.* Indeed, wherever there is a theology, or certain number not of definite precepts but of more or less definite propositions on speculative and historical topics, this confusion takes place in the minds of those who accept these doctrines as of unchangeable nature and unquestionable authority. To the theologians who condemned Galileo, the battle of faith concentrated itself upon the question whether the earth moved or not; *e pur si muove!* To many of the present day it seems a question of faith whether we accept or reject the Darwinian hypothesis as to the origin of man, and the genesis of things; and this false identification of faith and religion with a particular view of things, made in the first instance by the theologians, has been accepted by many men of natural science; who, seeing that the clerical view of things is condemned already within the whole possible circumference of science, have supposed Faith and Religion to be thereby exploded as irreconcilably at variance with science, or to have disappeared as prior and imperfect forerunners of positive knowledge.† A battle is being waged undoubtedly between various modes

* See in especial the "Notice to the Third Edition" of his "Gospel of the Resurrection."

† How misleading and unfortunate is Dr. Draper's *Title*: "The History of the Conflict between *Religion* and Science." London, 1875. The italics are mine.

of thought, various views of the Universe, of God, Man, and Nature: and these various modes of thought, though they all speak with equal definiteness, may be broadly classed as either theological or scientific or perhaps better said, as either dogmatic or critical. The history of thought shows nowhere clearer than since the development of physical science in modern times, that dogma is doomed to fall and criticism to triumph: were Faith interchangeable with dogmatic Theology, there are few if any more victories in store for Faith. But the battle of Faith is quite other than the process of deciding which of the two views of anything or all things is more probable; the battle of Faith is always and everywhere the same, its new victories are only the old victories which repeat themselves in every case where the spiritual life is begun and carried through by the grace of God. Selfishness and insanity are the only foes of Faith; and the salvation wrought in the ignorant or the outcast is the same, due to the same powers, as when the victory of Faith is achieved in the life of a Theologian, versed in disputes about various views of the Universe. It is something accidental, not essential in reference to Faith, whether a man concern himself with arguments and experiments, or with making screws; even granted that scientific ideas play a larger part in the general progress of mankind than screws do.

It is not our business in this place to follow out the practical bearings of this essential distinction between Faith as Religion and Faith as Theology; for the object of this Essay is not homiletical, but merely theoretic. Suffice it to observe that it is an untold gain for peace and disinterestedness of mind in a man, when once he sees that the disputes between various theoretic methods and conclusions are something quite different from the victory of Faith, in which latter the question at issue is as little the acceptance of any number of theoretical principles as the observance of a certain number of definite precepts.

THE END.